Inside the Team

Other Books on Leadership

Educational Leadership and Moral Literacy: The Dispositional Aims of Moral Leaders by Patrick M. Jenlink (2014) (978-1-61048-726-9)

The Tools of Leadership by Frederic W. Skoglund (2013) (978-1-4758-0523-9)

A Ten-Minute Approach to Educational Leadership: A Handbook of Insights for All Level Administrators by Robert Palestini (2013) (978-1-4758-0304-4)

Communicating Effectively: Tools for Educational Leaders, 2nd Edition by Michael B. Gilbert (2012) (978-1-61048-597-5)

Contours of Great Leadership: The Science, Art, and Wisdom of Outstanding Practice by Rosemary Papa, Fenwick English, Mary Culver, Ric Brown, and Frank Davidson (2012) (978-1-61048-830-3)

The School Improvement Planning Handbook: Getting Focused for Turnaround and Transition by Daniel L. Duke, Marsha Carr, and William Sterrett (2012) (978-1-61048-631-6)

Inside the Team

Questions and Answers Facing Teacher Leaders

Janet Burgess and Donna Bates

ROWMAN & LITTLEFIELD
Lanham • Boulder • New York • London

Published by Rowman & Littlefield
A wholly owned subsidiary of The Rowman & Littlefield Publishing Group, Inc.
4501 Forbes Boulevard, Suite 200, Lanham, Maryland 20706
www.rowman.com

16 Carlisle Street, London W1D 3BT, United Kingdom

Copyright © 2014 by Janet Burgess and Donna Bates

All rights reserved. No part of this book may be reproduced in any form or by any electronic or mechanical means, including information storage and retrieval systems, without written permission from the publisher, except by a reviewer who may quote passages in a review.

British Library Cataloguing in Publication Information Available

Library of Congress Cataloging-in-Publication Data Available

978-1-4758-1020-2 (cloth : alk. paper)
978-1-4758-1021-9 (pbk. : alk. paper)
978-1-4758-1022-6 (electronic)

∞ ™ The paper used in this publication meets the minimum requirements of American National Standard for Information Sciences Permanence of Paper for Printed Library Materials, ANSI/NISO Z39.48-1992.

Printed in the United States of America

Contents

Acknowledgments	vii
Foreword	ix
Jack Berckemeyer	
Preface	xi
1 Perspective	1
2 Leadership in Action	9
3 Dynamics and Leading Teams	27
4 The Focus on Practice	45
5 Shifts and Change	65
Appendix	79
References	97
Index	103
About the Authors	109

Acknowledgments

To the many teacher leaders, teachers, directors, and building administrators who asked questions and engaged in conversations with us around their practices, challenges, frustrations, conundrums, team insights, and myriad successes, thank you.

For those shared stories of working with students in this age of digital tools, an overwhelming abundance of information, and competing demands, thank you!

To Stephanie, Dotty, and Debbi in Washington; Aletia, Arturo, Joe, Garnetta, Randi, Tom, Ali, Beth, and K.D. in Oregon; James and Carole in California; Anna in Arizona; Jeff in Michigan; Shelley Joan in Wisconsin; Reggie and Ashley in Tennessee; Bob, Rob, and Cathy in Rhode Island; Joan in Pennsylvania; Mike and Chris in Maine; and to the teacher leaders and the teams we visited with in Oklahoma, Minnesota, Arizona, Oregon, and Utah, thanks for inviting us into your schools and classrooms and into your team conversations. You make answering team leader questions so easy and your professionalism does the business of education proud.

To our supportive, faithful Pete, Beth, Micki, Vicki, Jane, and Arturo, your feedback and insightful reading not only showed us gaps but pointed out why this book was needed. Thank you for your leadership and steadfast support through the years. It has been the project without end.

Finally, to our good friend Janet for your hospitality and for turning your dining room table over to us time and time again. This book wouldn't exist without you.

Foreword

Jack Berckemeyer

I have often wondered if, as teachers, we are just sitting on the park bench of life, with a box of chocolates, waiting for something or someone that is just right around the corner? Well, I think we have been sitting on that park bench far too long!

Across the decades, we have sought leadership from central office, school boards, principals, legislators, governors, mayors, state education departments, and our presidents. We have looked to these leaders to step up and provide us with the vision and the "how to" to get better results for our nation's children. This desire for leadership is as powerful as a working copy machine, a good cup of coffee, or an extra chicken nugget from the lunch ladies!

However, when it comes to real change and real reform, the educators who should be leading the way are the teachers and school leaders who are dealing with the never ending new, and sometimes radical, requests and mandates. It is time for our voices to be heard, and now is the time for teachers and school leaders to step up and answer the call of leadership. I am and always will be an advocate for teacher leadership and teacher empowerment. After reading *Inside the Team*, I have come to realize that teachers must work together to lead our schools and our teams.

The authors have provided the reader with amazing examples, outstanding scenarios, and mind-blowing conversational points that will push the most veteran educators and will truly inspire the struggling new teacher. For the reluctant emerging leader, this book is also for you. It helps you become a true change agent for your teams and for your school.

I would ask as you read this book, challenge yourself to look at your team and building-wide structures. While reading this book I learned a great deal about school and district-wide structures. It also made me reflect back on my own school district and on how the school superintendent that I worked for believed in site-based decision making. The site for all decision making was his office. The authors challenge that belief, and they ask you as the reader to be a voice of change.

The best part of this dynamic book is when the authors encourage you to set clear expectations and create a solid vision and implore you to build strong student relationships. They explore team dynamics, Common Core, and the ever changing issues of technology. The authors provide you with realistic ideas and solutions that allow you to reflect and refine your leadership skills. They enforce the power of teaming and the importance of student academic success. What more could you ask for in a leadership book? Plus you will love the analogy of the onion!

The authors are committed to teachers being a powerful voice in the educational process. They no longer want us to sit on the park bench and wait for someone to take our hand and walk us down the path of leadership. They want each of us to stand up on our own and take the leadership walk! Trust me. Take the walk to become a powerful teacher-team leader. You will never be the same after you complete this incredible journey.

Jack Berckemeyer
Educational Consultant, Author, and Humorist

Preface

The challenges of teaching and learning in this era of rapid change dominate conversations in educational communities across the nation. Technology, copious information accessible via the Internet to anyone at any time, the impact of the Internet on content acquisition, the imposition of Common Core Curriculum Standards, and the economy are all impacting the very nature of teaching and learning. Meanwhile the race for educating students who can work and compete in a global environment has become critically important.

Teachers are told be bold. Be innovative. Make a difference. Keep your focus. Oh, and work together. What goes unheard is: *How? How do I . . . ? How do we . . . ? What should I . . . ? What happens if . . . ? Is there a road map?* Many teachers are finding themselves in positions of leadership, and while not looking to move into administration, this role of leading peers has its upsides and downsides.

Whether selected, elected, or appointed in a formal leadership capacity or leading from an informal position of influence, perhaps presiding over a standing committee in a volunteer capacity, navigating the leadership role can be messy.

Where do teacher leaders turn for answers within context about leadership responsibilities and questions about professional practices when leading teams?

"As much as current educational leadership points to the need for teacher leadership, there is scant realistic material written by teacher leaders explaining *how* to be an effective teacher leader" (Gabriel, 2005, p. ix).

In response to this *how* question, Jan Burgess and Donna Bates wrote *Other Duties as Assigned: Tips, Tools and Techniques for Expert Teacher Leadership*. Published in 2010, this resource guide helps teacher leaders and others determine the skills, processes, and structures needed to build strong teams, whose mission is to guide student learning. Along the way, the reader would ponder leadership dilemmas as they were encouraged to reflect on their own leadership practices.

Many K–12 teacher leaders told us *Other Duties* helped them get started or adjust their work as leaders. However, questions continue to surface around the quandaries of peer leadership.

- I'm not an administrator, so how do I help us focus on what we do best, teaching, with no money, no time, and not really any power?
- How can I as teacher leader move the team's conversations forward to focus on teaching and learning for us, the adults, as well as students?
- How can a diverse group of teachers work together collaboratively and professionally? Where do team values play a part, or do they?
- Where do you go when the team is stuck in the past and thinks good enough is all right?

The authors combed through their collective sixty-plus years in public education and the approximately 1,620 team/leadership/department/cadre and cohort meetings they participated in, led, facilitated, observed, or troubleshot to answer the questions being asked and to provide context for those answers.

Inside the Team: Questions and Answers Facing Teacher Leaders revisits the concept of leadership, takes a collection of actual teacher-leader questions and offers approaches, conversation starters, strategies, and useful, practical tools teacher leaders and their teams can utilize to guide their journey toward successfully engaging colleagues in ways that impact students and learning.

The book is divided into five parts. The first part examines the multiple factors impacting education and the challenges these lay at the teacher leader's door. The remaining four look at universal quandaries teacher leaders face through a series of questions that end with conversation starters meant for reflection and dialog. Whether you are focusing on one question/scenario that reflects your current dilemma or reading the book straight through, the investment of time to reflect on your leadership and build a framework for peer and student success is a worthy endeavor.

Moving a team of peers (regardless of whether it's called an interdisciplinary team, a department, a grade level, a study group, or data analysis cadre) into critical and complex conversations that ultimately change professional practice can be the challenge.

Inside the Team asks teacher leaders to use their teams' structures and systems for the deep conversations that allow introspection, analysis, examination, questioning, and probing about professional practices, responsibilities, and teaching and learning for student growth. None of this happens without building trust, relationships, and a commitment to using the diverse strengths of the entire team.

Teacher leaders who are able to do this are in a pivotal position to bring a collaborative focus to dissect current practice, analyze the *whats*, *hows*, and *whys* inside classrooms and begin the conversation with their peers that can change or reshape teaching and learning practices to best meet student needs today. Along the way, the group learns to navigate through the demands that are changing the educational landscape.

Teacher leaders can make the difference between a highly functional and focused team and one swayed by circumstances, personalities, and the times. It takes more than good intentions from a team of professionals to address the complexities in educating each student successfully in today's changing educational climate. It takes leadership, a leadership construct that believes building strong relationships centered on teaching and learning is critical to help all students succeed.

Use the collection of questions and scenarios found in *Inside the Team* to find others who have faced the same dilemmas and quandaries that you and your team are grappling with, and use the resources, tools, conversation starters and advice to propel your professional work forward!

We hope our personal journey and our experience can help you and your team find your way more easily.

Safe journeys,
Jan and Donna

ONE

Perspective

Effective teacher leaders look at the trends and forces that impact teaching and learning and make strategic adjustments, navigating obstacles to keep the focus on what matters.

A METAPHOR FOR THE TIMES

Dear Jan: Our team is overwhelmed by so many changes and what is being asked of us. Right now, everything is curriculum and assessment, before that it was technology and a new online grading system, a year before it was integration and teaming. I need a way to take hold of all these various shifts and mandates and focus on what we can actually do that'll make a difference for the kids in our classrooms. Can you help me understand this crazy, changing world we're facing?

In schools the challenge is and always has been clear: What are you and your colleagues doing to ensure that student engagement and learning converge? That question isn't new; it's what schools, teachers, and teams are about. However, layer upon layer of policy, initiatives, and mandates, theory, practice, and people surround the students, the learners, at the heart of your question. These influences or triggers exist and do impact what happens inside that core (teaching and learning).

As the team's leader, to help answer your question and provide perspective for your team, first look at what constitutes those layers. It might help to visualize an onion. You notice the tough onion skin and if you cut the onion open, you see the many tight layers separated by thin membranes. You can slice open or peel the onion, layer by layer, until you reach the core. Each layer brings you closer to what comprises the center of this particular vegetable. If your eyes have stopped watering from the strong juice of the onion, notice the many ring layers that comprise the whole onion. In the center is the seed.

Today's twenty-first-century school is very much like an onion with layers of complexity that can be peeled away and examined layer by layer so their influence and impact on the core can be identified. The core of any educational model is successful student learning. Each layer that surrounds the student is significant. As a teacher leader, have your team examine each layer named above to understand the impact and the challenges each has on teacher practice and on successful student learning.

In an ideal world, the onion is an expensive, small, flavorful shallot, tight, firm, a few layers thick. Today, however, that onion is a late harvest Walla Walla Sweet or Vidalia with a tough outer skin, many thick layers with thin membranes that allow the juices to soak into the core. Slicing this onion open can make you weep.

It may help you dissect the layers of today's proverbial education onion and look at the challenges each imposes on your leadership and on what happens in your classrooms.

The first layer of this educational onion are the outside forces that are impacting our society and our lives. Primary here is technology. Yesterday's world was filled with local news, local activities and with students studying and learning in individual classrooms. Like the smell of a strong onion on our senses, technology hit us where we live and changed the face of the world forever. Local became global, social media opened communications around the globe, texting connected people instantaneously, information was available from multiple sources, and all of us could surf the web anytime, anyplace and for whatever interested us!

Today most of us carry one or more digital devices with us wherever we go. Some carry computers, others a cell phone, and still others devices with applications that can direct our driving routes or even allow us to order dinner while landing in an airport miles from home. So it is with our students. They too are constantly using these devices to help them learn and to help them connect to others in ways many adults cannot even being to imagine.

The impact technology has had on our school organizational model and our methods, from research and learning to curriculum offerings and data gathering and recording, is staggering. The challenge is to educate students living in a world buffeted by the explosion of technology, while keeping up with the explosion of devices and tools teachers are expected to utilize.

A shift from studying the world from a dated textbook to studying a dynamic and changing world by identifying problems and issues, across all discipline areas, has become the new textbook of the twenty-first-century school, truly classrooms without walls.

These changes are the result of technology. The challenge for teacher leaders and their teams is to identify and implement teaching and learning strategies that engage students in content where there are multiple entry points for such studies. When teachers harness technology, learning can become more personalized, connecting students to the content they study. Finding the time to learn which tools and which practices are most effective is another challenge teacher leaders and teams must grapple with.

The second layer of this onion in today's educational system is pedagogical in nature. The national focus on content standards, accountability, assessment, or other policy impacts the entire system. Common Core State Standards (CCSS) define not only what students should know and be able to do to succeed in postsecondary studies, work, and life, but also how well. Working to embed those standards into the curriculum and into meaningful instruction has impacted what teachers teach and what they do and challenges traditional practices.

Actually, the Common Core State Standards are an onion in their own right with layers of information, skills, and subsets that drill down to lessons, activities, strategies, and practices that affect teaching and learning in every classroom.

When standards are analyzed and used to pinpoint skills, knowledge, and concepts to be learned, teacher leaders and their teams can use them as the *what* of teaching, blending the *hows*, *wheres*, *whys*, and *whens* into a conceptual model that is engaging to students, uses a variety of tools and strategies, and makes learning irresistible.

The challenge for teacher leaders is to find the time to understand how to use standards in a way that supports and enhances their teaching to meet the learning needs of their students. Massive amounts of useful information and resource materials are available online and the wise teacher leader understands he does not have to reinvent the wheel. Take what's there and modify it to be useful.

Unfortunately, the CCSS are only one of many initiatives and federal, state, or district mandates impacting schools today. Teacher leaders must help navigate these various targets and find a way to categorize and prioritize them.

The third layer of the onion is the expanding body of research available to professionals. A substantial body of qualitative, quantitative, and longitudinal research studies and results exists that can and should inform practice. As Marzano, Pickering, and Pollock (2001) note, "Research provides remarkably clear guidance as to the steps schools can take to be highly effective in enhancing student achievement" (p. 11).

Research findings help practitioners answer the question "What works?" Research documents effective practices, strategies, and techniques that facilitate learning as well as debunks unsubstantiated, but often prized, techniques or activities. Teacher leaders can help their colleagues ask "So what now?" and investigate that research for solutions.

Research coupled with definitive knowledge about the brain that details how students learn should inform the work being done by teachers and their teams in schools across the country. Turning research into practice, having the time to learn and implement these research-based effective practices while working with each other, has caused teachers and schools to reexamine long held beliefs, like class credits and grading versus proficiency and flex time.

Respected researchers and educators have teamed up to provide clear and compelling models that will impact student achievement if studied and implemented with fidelity. The challenge to teacher leaders and their teams is to use their time to focus on student data, to research effective practices and strategies, and to find and implement those best practices that are effective teaching each and every student.

The fourth layer is the various organizational structures available that support learning. No longer do students learn only when in a traditional brick and mortar school; information and knowledge is a simple finger click away. Digital devices, instant communication, and avenues for learning compete with "school" in some instances. From home schooling to charter schools, online schools, and magnet schools to blended-learning high schools with college credit opportunities, to community schools built around sustainable ecological practices, the plethora can be staggering.

The challenge for teachers and teams is to harness those other avenues of learning and engage students in ways that make coming to school and staying in school meaningful. That means teachers need to inspect what happens in each individual and group of classrooms, find ways to operate across the team, draw on students' interests, and build choices and learning opportunities that allow all students to discover their unique talents while ensuring all reach a level of performance that will allow them to be successful outside the school environment.

Professional structures are in flux as well. Professional Learning Communities, or PLCs, are the current rage, just as interdisciplinary teams and departments once were. Teacher leaders used to be generalists; today many are anointed for their expertise to lead a group of peers for a specific task. Often these groups have little money or time for their work. Those constraints shouldn't negate the value of the structure; rather, it demands to be defined, focused, and productive. The challenge is for teacher leaders to define their leadership and keep the focus on professional growth and support.

The fifth layer is the shift to the belief that all students can and will be successful. It is at this layer that the teaching-learning paradigm becomes evident. Instructional strategies, practices, approaches, and pedagogy influence the core (students and learning). Just as Mastery Learning once inhabited this layer, today a framework like the Framework for Student Centered Learning (see Tool 1.1 in appendix) puts all students at the center of teaching and learning, with success for ALL adding complexity and challenging traditional practices.

The shift to a student-centered learning approach invites all students to participate and supports the notion that all students should be fully engaged in learning. Collaborating with others locally, nationally, and across the globe becomes a foundation for sustaining meaningful learning that is problem based, so all students participate.

In this scenario, schools are places where answers to problems are explored and where viable solutions are discussed. Learning communities must be places where ideas frame the content, where thinking is critical to learning, where cultural lines are blended, where diversity is embraced, and where collaboration is critical to sustaining personalized learning environments. The challenge is to commit fully to the belief that all students will and can learn and live that belief through words and actions each and every day.

The sixth layer is the educators, closest to the core. The administrators, the support staff, the teachers, and teams all work to support students in their quest to achieve academic success. Working together, these educators provide the direction and the support needed for students to reach their highest academic potential. As the policies and federal, state, and local requirements increase, it takes additional hands to move forward and to keep the focus on students' teaching and learning.

It's here that teacher leaders and teams working collaboratively and with focus help maximize a school's effectiveness in reaching all its clientele. They do this when they share ideas, use research-based best practices, match learning interests with natural interests, and work to develop and maintain a trusting partnership with students; as they all work toward reaching the same goal, learning becomes irresistible. The challenge to teacher leaders is to keep the team's focus on teaching and learning, as much for the adults on the team as for the students in the classrooms.

The center of the proverbial onion is the students. They are the heart of the educational endeavor. All other layers are working with each student to build their skills, knowledge, and capacity to learn and grow now and into the future. The center, these students in schools today, hold the keys to the future.

In today's fast-paced and information-rich world, many students bring a different mindset to school. The culture has changed, how information and knowledge is accessed has changed, the ability to flourish as learners has changed. Whether asked to embed the tools of technology into curriculum or help change the culture of a school or team to one that values and supports collaboration and critical thinking, school leaders must help their various publics understand the impact the onion layers have and use them, along with professional expertise, to blend and/or refine teaching and learning practices so all students are successful, now and into the future.

The challenge for teachers and teams is to understand how those changes impact their work and how they affect the future, navigate the swirling waters, and keep focused on building professional support so teaching and learning is strengthened. That means developing a bit of tough onion skin, not letting the juices cause you to weep and wring your hands but to see the whole, keep change in perspective, and be strategic in prioritizing your focus.

In today's world where information and communication arrive at nanosecond speed, change is a constant—which change is commanding attention at any moment is the variable. How teachers and teacher teams peel the layers away and use those changes to engage students will determine how successful students will be as they move confidently and competently into the future.

In today's schools, every student counts, every student deserves the best education they can possibly receive and feel valued in the process. How you ensure that student engagement and learning converge is the challenge. Leadership, building relationships to support each other and strengthen what you do and how you do it, is one answer.

In the end, it comes down to using your organizational structure, the team, to focus your work together to understand the prevailing shifts and trends, how they impact teaching and learning and the students you encounter, and find the intersections that will strengthen teaching practices and engage all students in learning. Ask yourself, so now what? What window of opportunity does this open?

The core of the onion never changes, only the layers do. When those layers are peeled away exposing students and learning, you've arrived at the true heart of your work as a team.

CONVERSATION STARTER

1. Draw an onion with five or six layers and ask team members to label what they believe are the critical components that surround the core. Start by first identifying what your core is and label out from there. How are the various onion layers impacting the work you do in your classroom or with the team? Are there any layers that you question or are resisting currently? Why? How is this manifesting itself in practice? Does it support the work you are doing to impact the core?
2. Who is the person you ask, "Help me think this through" as you grapple with whatever charge you have as teacher leader? Identify that support; you'll want to keep it nearby as leaders are sometimes the target of "Why me's," "This isn't fair," and "You're the leader, you do it."

3. Share the Framework for Student Centered Learning Environments with your team and identify which elements are currently in place, how they manifest themselves, and which element, if any, the team would like to investigate.

ADDITIONAL INFORMATION ON PERSPECTIVE

- "Redesigning Professional Development," *Educational Leadership*, 2002, 59(6) p. 195 is worth reading to get a perspective about working with teams and changing practices.
- "Teaching for the 21st Century" (September, 2009). Note: This edition of *Educational Leadership*, coupled with *Curriculum 21* (Jacobs, 2010), presents a compelling case for how students learn and how teachers approach the learning needs of students.
- *The Teaching Gap*, James W. Stigler and James Hiebert (1999). Note: this book is important because it recognizes that to improve student learning, the focus must shift to how teachers teach. It's in the process of improving teaching that learning is impacted. This easy to read book goes to the core of what happens in classrooms that make a difference in teaching for learning.

TWO

Leadership in Action

Effective teacher leaders create the conditions for others' success by building strong relationships to support their focus on teaching and learning.

THE POWER OF LEADERSHIP

Dear Jan: In our school, our leadership group and the principal meet a lot and he shares things we're to keep secret. Recently, he had some confidential information about a student and again we were sworn to secrecy. This isn't the only example of our group becoming exclusive; it isn't conducive to what we're about. How can the issues of trust and information be addressed?

Sometimes information is kept confidential. There may be several reasons for this; legal requirements, to build power, or being unaware of the impact that has on collegial work. How information is used, shared, or kept can create a climate of exclusion or inclusion. Secrets change the operating dynamics of any organization, as your question shows.

The old adage that "information is power" holds true in all organizations. Some leaders grab on to that power to raise their own status and to have control over people and use information for their own gain. Hoarding information can be a barrier to trust and to building a community that works together.

For leadership to be productive at any level, leaders must reach out and mobilize every single person in the organization. There is no place for power hoarding when building for success. Leaders who create the conditions for others' success build capacity throughout an entire organization by developing systems and structures to put information in the hands of all those affected. That helps break down barriers, isolation, and exclusion, so the organization becomes effective and efficient.

Effective leaders at all levels of the organization understand that trust becomes the glue to both personal and professional relationships. How you get those results matters more than who gets the results.

Sharing information within and across the organization signals a trust that we are all in this together because the business of school leadership and leadership teams is ultimately about creating the conditions for successfully moving the teaching and learning agenda forward.

Unfortunately, there are examples of administrators and teacher leaders who use information to leverage their own status. That ultimately creates that sense, real or imagined, of exclusion.

To change that, effective leaders know it's critical to develop a culture based on honesty, a clear sense of purpose, and relationships that are both personal and professional and to share information in a timely fashion and regularly assess the temperature, the mood, of the organization. Leaders know that when everyone is on the same page, momentum occurs.

In *The Skillful Leader: Confronting Mediocre Teaching*, Platt, Tripp, Ogden and Fraser (2002) remind us, "Real, day-to-day leadership for change, however, means working from the inside to influence the culture of the organization and the behavior of its members" (p. 3).

As a teacher leader, this is where you and your cohorts step in. You should be able to ask and answer the following questions:

- What is our leadership structure? Does it work so we operate in a fluid, flexible, open manner? If not, what needs to change?
- What is our purpose/mission/goal? Do we all know this and own it?
- Do we gather input, suggestions, questions, and concerns across the organization? How or why not?
- What barriers do we face in our overall organization that could slow down or derail communication?
- Are our leadership roles clearly defined? What are their purposes?
- Have we built a culture of openness and trust? How do we know?
- What systems do we have in place to share information, for meeting agendas and outcomes from leadership and other team meetings across the organization? Is this done regularly and consistently?

Teacher leaders understand that sometimes their role involves risk, particularly the risk to question things that feel off-kilter. Questioning should be done respectfully, in person, and is best when it's in a one-to-one conversation. Yes, the time and place to bring issues and questions up is important, so you might want to rehearse what you'll say and make an appointment to share your concerns.

Researchers Marzano, Waters, and McNulty (2005) found, "Whether a school operates effectively or not increases or decreases a student's chances of academic success" (p. 3). In today's educational world, with so many pressures to succeed, it takes an entire organization working well together for the same purposes not only to survive but also to flourish. Taking a risk to bring up issues when things don't feel quite right is critical to move an organization forward.

"Good communication is a critical feature of any endeavor in which people work in close proximity for a common purpose," Marzano et al. (2005, p. 46) point out. That is particularly true when creating a culture of collaboration to meet the learning needs of all students. Establishing and fostering clear lines of communication to and from staff and within the staff are essential to build trust. Shared information is power.

In an effective school organization, here's how that might look.

- Meeting agendas are communicated in a timely fashion across the organization.
- Each meeting ends with a set of talking points that can be shared throughout the organization with fidelity.
- All meetings open; everyone knows she is welcome to sit in and observe any leadership meeting. A participant works through her teacher leader if issues or questions arise after the leaders disperse.
- Members of the faculty meet regularly to pinpoint shortcomings, ask questions, dispel rumors, and identify stresses.
- These are acknowledged and brought to the attention of the leadership group, inviting more dialog and suggestions for potential solutions.
- If information is confidential, that is acknowledged and the team working with that situation or issue is defined.

In all cases, the leaders from administrators to teacher leaders are clear about the purpose of the organization and keep that as the focus of the work of the entire group. Skilled leaders are also intentional about finding time and venues to build personal and professional connections across the organization, as they know everyone has talents and strengths. That commitment to tap into strengths across the organization makes teaching, learning, and leading stronger.

Looking at how leaders operate in your individual situation can be illuminating. Ask someone not in the leadership cadre what they see, feel, or expect and compare perspectives. Finding the points of intersection or agreement can help you decide what you can do or are willing to do.

In answer to your scenario about keeping student information confidential, rather than bringing up issues of exclusivity in a faculty meeting or complaining to a colleague in the parking lot, start with a conversation with the principal so he isn't blindsided. Then, if at all possible, the two of you should make plans to bring the issue to the attention of the leadership cadre because others may or may not be sensing this "insider versus outsider" dynamic. To function as a team, it will be important to get to the root of the issue so the organization can move forward.

Identify the concern and how it is affecting the work of the organization and seek additional perspectives before making a plan to address the issue. With a plan in mind, have that important conversation with the principal and others on the leadership team. You might find yourself surprised to find others see this issue as well and are ready.

Finally, think about your own leadership. Have you worked with highly effective leaders in the past? What attributes defined their leadership and which of those are you emulating? Then identify the things over which you have control and how you create the conditions for others to be successful. Talk with your group, your team, share your insights about leadership and inclusivity and monitor the systems and structures you've put in place that help you build that supportive, collaborative working group. Success breeds success, it starts with you.

STRUCTURES FOR PROFESSIONAL LEARNING

Dear Jan: I've been on so many different kinds of teams during my 24 years of teaching and now we're moving to Professional Learning Communities, a district mandate. I'm comfortable partnering with my English teacher colleague so I'm wondering why these are supposed to be better?

It's not what it's called, it's what you do that counts. Any number and variety of structures can be vehicles for collaborative inquiry, the deep conversations that allow introspective, data collection and analysis, and the examination and strengthening of professional practice. The names and composition may vary but when the purpose is clear and everyone owns the mission, the same components are needed for success as you experienced with your English teacher partner.

You enjoyed a successful two-person partnership or dyad. Creating that relationship took time to build trust and learn how each other operated before getting into the heart of how you teach. You'll find that holds true for the Professional Learning Community (PLC) structure. The name is different, not what it's for, and that is cause for celebration.

As you've found out, in any successful structure, there must be time to build relationships, to share practices and strengths, and to get to know one another as colleagues and professionals. That allows you to talk about teaching and learning practices, to find common points of agreement, and to share areas of difference. It is still a purpose-driven avenue to look deeply into practice.

If a collection of practitioners are randomly put together into PLCs with no common focus or goals and simply told "you are now a professional learning team, use your time to make a difference," it could be folly. On the other hand, with leadership, that kind of loose direction might allow the group the flexibility to come up with a variety of ways to work together, design the areas for professional inquiry based on the group's needs and wants, for instance, and carry out investigations of practice together.

In any case, what the group does and how it operates must be made clear; otherwise, yes, this new PLC structure could simply dissolve into a group of separate individuals who get no further than meeting with frustration. Defining those group norms and responsibilities from the outset is the role of the teacher leader as well as the group.

Here are some ways for you to identify how the PLC might be a useful and workable structure. When the new PLC does meet, see if the purpose is clearly defined, if the focus is on students and sharing exemplary practice, as well as what role individuals will have, how you are to work together, what support will be available and decide how you will participate from there. Perhaps others have examples of successful teaching partnerships to share. Some teachers may have been part of an interdisciplinary team or a department, with stories of collaboration and insights about what worked and what didn't.

What matters in the group is to understand the purpose (a community of learners who will look at strengthening or changing practices to meet the needs of students), what roles each individual will play, and how various successful experiences from the past inform or shape the functioning of the group.

Be patient; give the group time to develop the trust to have open and honest conversations. Work with the PLC's teacher leader to move the conversations into the direction of professional growth and development, and allow connections and collaborations to emerge. This will develop over time.

When forming a new Professional Learning Community, group members have a professional responsibility to:

- be active participants;
- be willing to share personally and professionally;
- commit to the work of the group;
- talk about practice in an intellectual, not emotional, manner;
- help define and modify goals as appropriate;
- give and receive feedback without making personal attacks;
- be supportive and collaborative, ask clarifying questions;
- listen without thinking of a quick rebuttal; and
- practice patience and work together to resolve problems by focusing on the larger goals.

There are instruments that can help the group look at the structure and elements that play a part as you work together. Use the National School Reform Faculty's Professional Learning Communities Survey, Tool 2.1 in the appendix, to pinpoint critical elements of your work and later as a survey instrument to check how the group is operating within the various dimensions. This reflection will help the PLC grow as a team. The Tool is available online at http://www.nsrfharmony.org/protocol/doc/plc_survey_exercise.pdf or http://www.nsrfharmony.org/protocol/doc/plc_survey.pdf.

This survey and other protocols are invaluable as they help guide and put structure to conversations. Share this site with the PLC leadership. It can mean the difference between a group that is effective learning together or a group without direction.

Remember your empathy for how students feel as they move in and out of diverse learning groups. Some learn best by themselves, others need a group to help process information and knowledge, and still others prefer hands-on, experiential activities to see the bigger picture and assimilate concepts and knowledge.

Adults, too, have learning preferences and can be reticent about trying something new. As a veteran teacher, use this transition from a dyad to the PLC model you find yourself in to get perspective and to reflect on your practice. Learning is continuous; it just comes in different forms and in a variety of vehicles.

You've seen changes over time; some were effective, others not so much. When the focus of this PLC is on gathering evidence about current practice to strengthen the teaching practices of the whole team so all students are successful, jump in and help move the work forward. This work doesn't preclude your personal and professional relationship with that English teacher partner! Expect to find your work is fulfilling and engaging. Leadership and focus are the keys.

AN ACADEMIC CHALLENGE

Dear Jan: Our department has been challenged by several parents of talented and gifted students recently, saying we aren't giving their students enough high level work. We disagree, of course, as we really have been focused on working across concepts and doing small group work to help all our students reach these learning goals. However, apparently we haven't gotten that message across very well and now this response from some parents really has us wondering. Can you help?

This is a perfect opportunity to put the definition of your leadership into action on two fronts. First, relationships. As you've built those with your team to talk about teaching and learning, let's assume you have discussed ways each of you meet the challenge for gifted learners. Continue to have that important team conversation in light of a parent's question so you have a solid idea of how everyone does indeed position rigor in their practice.

Now begin to build solid relationships with the parents of these students. Reach out to them, meet with them, ask them to define more specifically their concerns, what had happened in the past that worked, what would they like to see different, and what they hope for for their children. Ask if they understand how you are building rigor and meaning into your conceptual approach, if indeed that is the work you are doing. How is that manifesting itself, and show the parents examples.

Does your district or school have a person whose responsibility it is to work with the talented and gifted population? Bring that person into the conversation with parents and with your team. Do TAG (talented and gifted) students have written plans so that goals are set to meet each learner's individual needs? How are those created? Who is in that conversation?

See where I'm going with this. Communication and information, access and respect are all part of building relationships so that everyone is creating the best environment for success for the students as learners. Again, this isn't a one-meeting connection but a genuine opportunity to build relationships to understand what the teachers do to offer challenging learning to all students.

The second part of this leadership definition is the focus on teaching and learning so all are successful. Within the team, how are teachers differentiating content, process, and products? Who has expertise in compacting curriculum and can share that knowledge with the others? Who has conceptual teaching expertise and can help everyone write essential questions that cover several disciplines and allow extensions, enhanced projects, simulations, or contracts be written that are choices students can take on to add complexity to their work?

These meaningful, focused conversations take your leadership. Pinpointing strategies to provide challenge and rigor in the practices in every classroom and putting those in writing so parents, students, and other teams or groups are aware of how you are addressing this critical area is not only your best defense but is your best offense. Keep the team from becoming defensive and seeing this complaint as a challenge. Find the windows of opportunity this opens and intentionally point that out.

You'll need to be strategic to keep a balance within the team as you also reach out to parents, but you are positioning your team for optimizing everyone's talents to build success. The other part of this is to share with the parents, in fact with all parents, how your team approaches rigor in your academic curriculum.

Rigor and relevance may be the buzzwords but the concepts are timeless. Here's what the parents want: academic rigor that challenges students to work at higher levels of cognitive processing and to move beyond memorizing and preparing for tests and working with content that is conceptual, engaging, and challenging.

As teachers, you want to provide a rigorous curriculum that teaches students to actively utilize their minds in critical and creative thinking as they work with knowledge, skills, and concepts that help them connect ideas across all content disciplines.

In such a curriculum, the learning focus shifts from studying a topic to one where students use multiple content sources that cross disciplinary lines. The goal is to analyze problems, consider possible solutions, look for patterns, or make connections between ideas and content while working with real problems and issues found in the world of today.

Students are encouraged to ask "why" or "what if" and to seek solutions to solve problems and suggest solutions using their understanding of how things work in different content domains. Finding meaning and relevance challenges students to work hard, persist when answers are unclear, and hopefully become deeply engaged in learning.

That's what parents want to see happen for their youngsters as well.

In essence, it comes down to this:

- What are you and your colleagues doing that provides these learning opportunities for your students?
- What content processes and demonstrations of learning are available and how do students access them?
- What choices do students have in how, when, and what they are learning?
- Do parents and students know this?

You indicate in your question that you are working across concepts; what does that look like and who knows this? Can you be explicit in how you are approaching this and what parents and students can expect? Have you shared the rigor and relevance material from the CCSS materials so parents understand what you aim for and how this pays out in the classroom?

There are so many projects, activities, and materials available on the Internet that support curricula that a wise teacher leader doesn't have to reinvent the wheel but uses what's been successful and modifies it to fit the work he or she is doing and extends, stretches, and enhances the work being done in the classroom.

As you move forward, a critical part of constructing or planning this kind of rigorous curriculum is teacher understanding and expertise. Linda Darling-Hammond (1998) states,

> First teachers need to understand subject matter deeply and flexibly, so they can help students create cognitive maps, relate ideas one to another, and address misconceptions. Teachers need to see how ideas connect across fields to everyday lives. Teachers must be able to use different teaching strategies to accomplish various goals and means for evaluating students' knowledge and assessing students' approaches to learning. Finally, teachers need to be able to analyze and reflect on their

practice, to assess the effects of their teaching and to refine and improve their instruction. (p. 6)

As teacher leader, here is your mindset. Teachers must be content experts who work together collaboratively to design and implement instruction that challenges students to actively utilize their minds in creative and critical thinking, to examine content, analyze problems, consider possible solutions, look for patterns, or make connections between ideas and concepts. The model for learning recognizes students enter school with different skills, abilities, backgrounds, and life experiences.

The learning focus shifts from learning about a topic to one where students use content information to help them understand the *hows* and *whys* of their world. This results in differentiated curriculum and instruction, challenging all students to high levels of engagement and learning.

As a teacher leader, have the team develop a response to the parents' challenge by analyzing your approaches to differentiation and examine the practices you use to ensure high levels of engagement and thinking. You might use Tool 2.2 in the appendix, Taking Promising High School Practices to Scale to jumpstart this critical conversation among team members as you think about what you have going on that meets this requirement for rigor.

Then develop specific team supported informational materials that explain to the entire parent community your approach to teaching and learning, what constitutes rigor in your curriculum, and how you approach differentiation. Putting these in writing makes you be specific and succinct. Watch out for "educationese"; be clear and talk about practices for both intellectual challenge and ongoing support.

Consider sharing this important information through

- parent information nights;
- student demonstration nights with exemplary work on display and shared by students;
- student-led parent conferences where skills, knowledge, and concepts take center stage;
- team or department handouts that identify the common skills, knowledge, concepts, and big themes students will work with over a trimester, semester, or year with the essential questions identified; and
- Open House Information Nights where you share the Promising Practices Table (Tool 2.2) and your curriculum anchor standards along with the key themes, content strands, strategies and learning targets you have designed for your students; demonstrate how students can work at varying levels of difficulty to reach these goals.

By approaching this challenge through the two leadership prongs, building relationships and focusing on teaching and learning together, parents will have a better understanding of how you approach teaching and student learning needs to challenge all students. Plus, the team of teachers you work with will have a better grasp of what's happening currently and which emerging practices they can target for professional growth so that you are indeed offering a rigorous learning experience for students.

Need a few quick ideas? Be sure to check out the American Association of School Librarians website, as that has a multitude of projects at varying levels of complexity.

A TESTING/PACING DISAGREEMENT

Dear Jan: I'm having a running battle with my administration. We're expected to teach, test, reteach, retest and make sure all our kids reach 80 percent mastery before we move on! On top of that, we are to follow a pacing guide that doesn't take into account either my expertise or the pace of kids learning. What happened to giving me the professional courtesy to know what I'm doing?

This is a question we've been hearing the last couple years from teacher leaders and teams across the country as accountability and test scores seem to be driving many conversations. This onion layer, test scores and the practice of assessment, is currently in a position of importance.

So understanding what it is and what this means will give you some perspective. Assessment provides information that directs or refocuses learning, or at least that's the idea behind using test scores (assessment) to measure learning. But for assessment to be useful to guide teachers in instruction and students in their learning, it must come as immediate and meaningful feedback. And therein lies the conundrum, as you clearly know.

A district is accountable to their stakeholders for who's learning and at what level (summative assessment), using test scores for that purpose, while teachers use assessment to diagnose and guide student learning (formative assessment). Clearly communicating these differences, in essence stating the purpose for the assessment, is one answer, as these are two sides of the same "accountable for learning" coin.

Both are important, so it's probably the instructional learning time lost in all that testing that is really the issue. With the push toward standardized testing based on common standards, both administrators and teachers are working to find a balance between the formal tests students will be required to take, ones that show how much they have learned (summative), and those ongoing checks for understanding that take place in the classroom on a daily basis that direct learning (formative).

Using the common core standards as the learning targets for students, teachers must find a way to connect the two types of assessment: formal, standardized tests that are accountability measures (how well students are learning the intended curriculum) and informal assessments (to direct student learning). That approach uses assessment as another tool in the toolbox to direct and support learning while working with accountability, a state and federal requirement. That might not sound like the answer you want; however, it is the reality of today's educational milieu.

To that end, employing multiple tools to assess the knowledge gaps between instruction and student learning outcomes allows teachers to set a learning plan for each student or group of students. When target learning goals are set, both teacher and student know the path learning will take and both know what needs to be done to reach the target.

Personalized learning plans where the interests, skills, and knowledge of students coalesce into active learning opportunities best suited for each student or groups of students is the answer to a balance between formal assessments and ongoing classroom progress checks. This way, the entire class doesn't stop working if a small group hasn't mastered a skill.

So, when the school's or district's directive is for each and every student to reach a certain level of skill before moving forward, your first option once a student hits that magic mastery number, be it 80 percent, 90 percent, or 100 percent, is to identify options available so the student can deepen his or her work in a way that broadens the connections with real world problems or across content while others are working toward those learning targets. That frees you up to pull the other students into small groups for reteaching and individual attention.

You are fighting a losing battle if you think testing will magically go away. What you can control are choices for extensions, contracting choices for projects and enrichment, reteaching by skills with various computer programs, and providing ongoing scaffolding which can be incorporated into your instruction so everyone reaches mastery.

Many teachers identify the skills and concepts that must be mastered and design differentiated lessons using them as a base. That way, all students can move at their own pace and build knowledge along the way. There are a plethora of excellent materials available for differentiation, both as professional development opportunities and as online projects you might consider.

Have you looked into the website for interesting projects and extensions? The resources and materials are extensive and, if not exactly what you want/need, you can ask who else is working on a particular concept or skill and begin a critical conversation that will guide your work.

Here's where you can balance the assessments with your teacher expertise and creativity. Alter what students are expected to do in three critical areas as detailed in Tool 2.3, Framing Content, Process and Product (see the appendix). Those areas include:

- Content—the kind of and how much content a student studies;
- Process—the way in which the student learns; and

- Product—the nature of how the student demonstrates learning.

Modifying or extending content and giving choices in how students learn and in ways they demonstrate their learning are yours to design and offer when a student has mastered the skills and knowledge expected by the district. Be as creative as you want as students are attracted to challenges that fit their style of learning, and this gives you time to work with those who need some extra coaching.

So while sometimes politics weighs in, you are still in control of how you teach, opening the door to be creative and flexible by broadening learning opportunities for all your students and using any variety of informal assessments that work for you and the students. This is one approach to your dilemma.

As for pacing charts, here are a couple of reactions. If the charts identify major concepts that must be taught and learned before the annual testing cycle, and you the teacher choose how and when to teach those concepts (using professional judgment and all you know about brain development, teaching, and learning) then pacing guides make sense.

If the pacing charts are in a daily or weekly lockstep approach, dictating which page and which lesson everyone must be on, and lessons must be taught regardless of how students are understanding the skills and concepts, then perhaps it's time to voice concern and bring your own analysis to those in charge in order to reexamine the purpose and effectiveness of pacing.

Respectfully, share your concerns with the learning experts using data (look at tests, timing, major skills, and concepts) and your research about learning and that you believe will better serve all students. Begin a much needed conversation; be collaborative and respectful without becoming militant, as that will stop anyone in a position of support from listening.

See if your team or department and teacher leader are with you and understand your concerns; be sure to work with the building's or district's instructional facilitator and perhaps district math committee. They surely had reasons for instituting a pacing guide. Have you asked what those were and how they came to be?

Your approach should be to convince others to assess the value of identifying major concepts after having analyzed the test questions so that teachers who are curriculum and developmental experts decide what is taught and when. It's not a radical change but one that is doable. The debate should center on student learning and their readiness to tackle intellectual content. Pacing here requires letting people absorb the ideas, data, and specific information and move in a new way. It can work; students' learning is at stake, so do your homework (analysis), find your voice, and stay the course.

Good teachers know good teaching. The realities of the day (see A Metaphor for our Times) must be taken into account. Remember who signs your paycheck; you aren't the Lone Ranger here, so work within the system to bring issues, concerns, and best practices forward. You might also enlist a third party, one who has the political capital, to advocate on your behalf. Yes, this approach takes time and thought, but then any meaningful change does.

EVALUATION AND FEEDBACK

Dear Jan: I'm a teacher leader and our leadership group meets monthly with our administration. Lately we've talked about having our team members give us feedback. I'm concerned this peer feedback will be used as an evaluation tool by the administration. My question is, are there assessments or rubrics already developed we might investigate that really are objective and maybe even help us grow as leaders? Second, do I approach the principal with my concern?

Implicit in your question are issues of trust and whether gathering peer feedback is a way to check on your performance as leader (evaluation) or whether peer feedback is a way to help you develop and grow as a leader (personal growth). Have you, as a teacher leader, asked the administrator whether this is feedback just for you or if it is to be shared?

Having this conversation within that group is important as it creates opportunities to clarify issues, concerns, and expectations and to answer questions openly and forthrightly. Ask what the purpose of the feedback is. Is it to evaluate your leadership or is it to help you learn and grow as a professional teacher leader?

There are roles and responsibilities implied in being a designated teacher leader with expectations for performance, even if those are poorly defined. Evaluating your performance might be an annual expectation, but it must be clear what the standards are for teacher leaders, what is expected, and what excellent teacher leaders do.

You can't aim high if you don't know what you are aiming for. Likewise, peers can't give feedback if they don't know what is expected from a teacher leader. For feedback to be helpful, it must be "goal referenced; tangible and transparent; actionable; user friendly (specific and personalized); timely; ongoing and consistent" (Wiggins, 2012, p. 13).

Evaluations of performance should be based on clear, measureable standards. Students who are evaluated know what the targets are; teacher leaders should be held to those same standards of objectivity.

If personal qualities like work ethic, vision, risk taking, and teaching skills are all part of the expectation for leaders, those qualities should be clearly spelled out and a fair assessment instrument (or instruments) should be developed that is understood and used regularly. Those assessments might include self-assessments, team feedback surveys, teacher-leader rubrics, problem scenarios as case studies, or portfolios of artifacts for each standard. However measured, teacher leaders must know what they are expected to do and at what level of performance.

Peer feedback, where you ask your colleagues how well you are meeting your various professional leadership roles, can lead to growth if done right. It is feedback

- that you ask for;
- that your colleagues understand is for your eyes only;
- that is confidential;
- that asks for examples in areas they have direct knowledge about; and
- that is for you to digest, consider and use to set goals or modify how you operate as a leader.

Feedback for these purposes is not part of an evaluation.

Here's a way to begin. First, is there a teacher leadership job description already developed in the district? If yes, take a look at it with your peers and see if there are clear definitions or standards that detail the skills and roles you are expected to play. Are performance standards defined as well? Any feedback or evaluation tool should be based on explicit, known standards so assessment is objective, just as you do with your students. It is only fair to know the targets, right?!

Second, if there are not clear definitions of your roles and responsibilities, ask the group of leaders and administrators to draft common expectations together. A written, shared teacher leadership set of standards is a district responsibility. If there aren't clear guidelines, it's possible your cadre of teacher leaders could take the lead and develop a set of roles with definitions you believe in. Work collaboratively with your administrator in developing these as that partnership will pay dividends in building trust and enhancing your professional respect.

Then, look for ways to develop a feedback instrument that is for your use as a teacher leader, one that is clear and objective and asks your peers for constructive feedback about what is working and pinpoints areas for possible growth. You are the owner of this information and can choose to share it with your administrator or not.

Consider piloting Tool 2.4 in the appendix, a sample Teacher Leaders Feedback Survey, with your team and see if the information you gather helps you set leadership goals or enhance your work with the team. You will get varying responses, most likely, as your peers have differing perspectives about your leadership.

Regardless, when you have this information, you then have an opportunity to think about what it means, how it will shape your work, and how and with whom you will share the results. You do share what you heard and describe how that will help you in the future.

Even if you get some feedback that says, "Here's an area to concentrate on because you need to refine/revamp/relook at it," take time to digest that feedback and see how you can use it to grow as a leader. It might not feel great to hear it at first, but true constructive criticism and feedback doesn't say you're a failure, it says some other areas now need your attention. Leaders have to stretch and grow, gather information and say to themselves, "Now what, what can I learn from this and how will it help me in the future?" And let's face it, as a teacher leader, you are learning so much and not all of it comes easily or naturally.

The real potential for personal growth as a leader comes from honest reflections from another perspective about how you are performing. Is your role a management one? More administrative? Instructionally focused? Are you a coach, facilitator, resource provider? When these roles are clear and when colleagues are asked to give feedback about what is working well and what needs strengthening, peer feedback can be highly informative and effective.

Collecting and using feedback should be seen as part of how we grow and learn as professionals. So in answer to your question, yes, there are instruments that are readily available to help you get started defining your roles and designing an objective feedback instrument. Here are three sources to start with:

1. Read and digest this outstanding research brief written by the esteemed Educational Testing Service, titled: "Teacher Leadership: An Assessment Framework for an Emerging Area of Professional Practice" available at http://www.ets.org/Media/Research/pdf/RR-10-27.pdf. Especially helpful in this report are the various ways to assess teacher leadership, and an example of a well-thought-out set of teacher leadership standards from Kansas found in Appendix A.
2. Wondering what the roles teacher leaders most often take on are? Read and refer to "Ten Roles for Teacher Leaders" by Cindy Harrison and Joellen Killion, ASCD, Sept. 2007, 65(1), pp. 74–77 online at http://www.ascd.org/publications/educational-leadership/sept07/vol65/num01/Ten-Roles-for-Teacher-Leaders.aspx. This will give you another list of skills to consider.
3. Finally, roles and responsibilities for teacher leaders are laid out in ASCD's (Association for Supervision and Curriculum Development) book *Other Duties as Assigned: Tips, Tools and Techniques for Expert Teacher Leadership*, particularly in pages 34–38, and the accompanying documents in the appendix by Burgess and Bates. This has a feedback document provided that you might consider as well.

Just as with students, for any feedback to be helpful, the feedback instrument must be developed ahead of time and everyone knows what is being asked, what the purpose is, and how it will be used and shared. Any feedback given should be specific and timely.

Then, in answer to the second part of your question, because the leadership team has discussed the difference between evaluations and feedback, trust that having a sincere and respectful conversation with the principal is in order as you talk about asking for and getting peer feedback. It is just that, feedback for your professional growth. You hope that, if each of you as a teacher leader is to be evaluated by the principal, it will be part of the annual evaluation cycle, based on specific job description and target goals that are known ahead of time and discussed together. That's your expectation as a professional.

CONVERSATION STARTERS

1. How do you define leadership? Describe the power structure at your school, how does it manifest itself? How does it impact your leadership?
2. Information is power; do you believe that? What systems do you have in place to share information in a timely, effective, and efficient manner? What needs to be adjusted? How do you know?
3. Did your team react to the academic challenge question posed in this section? Did you see yourselves in that scenario and if so, what did you find that will be useful as you craft your responses to parents and the community?
4. What conundrums are you or your team facing in terms of accountability for testing students or other mandates? Are you able to manage the pace of learning along with the tests needed to inform learning as well as meet school/district/state mandates? Is it possible to balance the two? Discuss this with team members. Where does differentiation fit into this equation? Describe how you are making this work. What do others do? Analyze ways to meet both needs while not giving up students' engagement with learning.
5. As teacher leader, do your team members know what it is you are responsible for and how your leadership will be evaluated? Do you solicit feedback from peers about your leadership on a regular basis? Why or why not? Knowing feedback impacts and pinpoints areas for growth, what conditions need to be in place for you to ask for feedback? Use the citations in the question to find potential instruments to use. Pilot one and see if it pinpoints areas for growth.

ADDITIONAL INFORMATION ON LEADERSHIP IN ACTION

- If you haven't read Wiggins's article "7 Keys to Effective Feedback" in *Education Leadership*, 70(1), Sept. 2012, pp.11–16, do so.

- "Teacher Leadership: An Assessment Framework for an Emerging Area of Professional Practice" available at http://www.ets.org/Media/Research/pdf/RR-10-27.pdf.
- Burgess and Bates provide a useful teacher leadership grid in *Other Duties as Assigned, Tips, Tools and Techniques for Expert Teacher Leadership*, 2009, that is easy to use and a great place to start looking at roles and responsibilities.
- *Educational Leadership*'s 2009 article by Charlotte Danielson, "Developing School Leaders," 67(2), p. 161 is an informative read.
- National School Reform Faculty/NSRF website is a treasure trove of useable protocols. Here are two examples: http://www.nsrfharmony.org/protocol/doc/plc_survey_exercise.pdf; and http://www.nsrfharmony.org/protocol/doc/plc_survey.pdf.
- TeachersPayTeachers.com, an open online source for shared teacher materials.

THREE
Dynamics and Leading Teams

Effective teacher leaders understand that schooling is a uniquely human endeavor and that relationships matter.

RELATIONSHIPS COUNT

Dear Jan: How important is it for my team to work on building relationships? For the most part we all like each other, so that's not a problem. Shouldn't we be focused more on the work we are doing with our students and not worry so much about team dynamics?

The more you are aware of and focus on the group's dynamics, the more successful you'll be in enhancing teaching and learning and providing support when the issues or conversations are tough. Let's look at that more closely.

Building team relationships is like learning content vocabulary; neither should occur in isolation, both need a framework to be meaningful. Whenever teachers ask their students to learn vocabulary in isolation, students learn word recognition. However, when students learn and use vocabulary within a content framework, meaning and conceptual understanding increases. Vocabulary then becomes a vehicle that connects discipline to discipline as students are able to think and talk about applications in other content areas.

In essence, for you and your group, you're building relationships while working together within a teaching/learning context.

Michael Fullan (2001), educational researcher and professor, wrote, "It is one of life's great ironies: schools are in the business of teaching and learning, yet they are terrible at learning from each other" (p. 92). He went on to say that if you get people to share about things they deem important, relationships deepen and learning takes place in the exchange.

For this to happen with a group of individual teachers, the group must know what they stand for (define your purpose) and develop a culture that will facilitate their work as a community.

As teacher leader, your role is to nurture the relationships that allow the team to delve deeply into current teaching and learning practices and to define together how you'll go about strengthen teaching practices so that all students are successful. As teacher leader, even if this is a one-project team, you nurture the group by intentionally asking others their opinions, listening, and providing arenas for conversations about who we are, what we believe, and how we operate. When you are genuinely interested in each person, others are, too.

The answers to these five questions will give you additional insights as to whether your team's relationships are strong enough to sustain the work you are asked to do:

1. Do we all know what our purpose is?
2. What values do we hold as a team?
3. Do each of us know what others bring to the team?
4. Have we talked about what kind of working environment best supports our work?
5. Have we grappled with what it means to put students at the center of our work together?

The real measure of a team's relationships is whether or not they can sustain deep, rich, critical conversations about strengthening team members' teaching and learning practices, making sure all students have someone who knows them well and who makes sure they are successful.

It all starts with establishing common understanding about the important work you've been charged with (investigate and begin working with a federal, state, or district mandate, say, or understand a new online grading system and begin using it), then develop goals, refine them with more specific sub-goals and set an action plan in place. Agree on who will do what and by when, share findings and insights, if appropriate pilot the new practice or strategy, and collect feedback and evaluate the results. It's the same implementation process you've used with PBIS (Positive Behavioral Intervention and Supports) or various new curriculum implementations.

By engaging in ongoing conversations that are purposeful and time centered, as a team you are building for student success. *We are here for our students!* becomes the purpose, focus, and reason for improving professional practice.

As you reflect on the group you are leading, consider:

- Do conversations about best teaching practices direct the work of the team?

- Are clear and honest communications central to the team's well-being?
- Is there a common commitment to everyone's success, students and teammates alike?
- Does your team have a set of core values you embrace? How do they manifest themselves on the team? With students?
- Are all voices heard and respected, or do differing or unique perspectives get dismissed?
- Is risk taking encouraged so support and feedback allow new ideas and practices to be examined?
- Is there commitment to work together on professional growth goals that are challenging and research based and will directly impact teaching and learning?

Here's a side note that is important. Effective teams who have built strong, trusting relationships know what their core values are and weigh decisions and issues against them. Core values define who you are, what you believe; they are sacred and nonnegotiable. Core values should ground the work your team does. Every one of you should know, understand, and use these critical values as you think about situations, dilemmas, questions, and their actions.

As teacher leader, take the time to hold this important conversation and use the following questions: What are the values the team holds as primary to its operations? Can you or your team members define core beliefs and values your group holds as nonnegotiable? Is trust one of your core values?

Consider using the Core Values Protocol, Tool 3.1 in the appendix, with your team to illuminate individual and collective values. Determining the team's core values is not a one-meeting conversation but a series of reflective exercises and focused conversations that should uncover the four or five shared values that ground your work that all team members subscribe to.

This exercise is worth the team's meeting time and the think time between meetings to engage in and sustain the work you are going to be doing together over time. To help cement strong personal and professional relationships within the group, it is an insightful undertaking. When differing points of view, issues, or dilemmas come up or new projects are proposed, you can use your core values as a lens through which to view and respond.

Recognizing and validating the individual work of team members is critically important. Every member brings interest, experience, and skills to the team table. A strong team is built collectively and purposefully, valuing the contributions of all. Your work on building team relationships is key to effectively strengthening the work all team members do so all students are successful; it's that simple. Remember there are two critical parts to leadership: people and purposeful work. They go hand in hand.

EMOTIONS AND BARRIERS

Dear Jan: How can I help move my team beyond emotional reactions to decisions and issues so we can actually talk through them and move forward? We keep reaching an impasse, then teachers align with one another or things get heated so we change the subject. I'd like ways to be proactive and productive. Got any suggestions?

Emotions are feelings that have gotten stirred up and provide a signal that a disturbance has happened. A strong, emotional reaction is a sign some significant issue has been touched. When emotions take over a discussion, whether it's exuberance, resistance, or anger, objectivity can be compromised.

Teams are like families in many ways; conflicts and differences will arise on occasion. The skilled leader will anticipate the issues that might be highly charged. The effective leader will know team members well enough to plan ahead and have in mind how to work through these people issues.

Change can be threatening; it might mean giving up something that could be valued, like time with family, or uncoupling a strong partnership for something unknown. Regardless, those emotions should be acknowledged; others don't have to agree but being heard makes a difference.

The first step is to cultivate relationships among the team members so that it is safe to express emotions and trust that people's responses will be considered and acknowledged for what they are. As the leader, ensure that processes are in place to help the group respond respectfully and move through these issues.

How to you plan for this? Anticipate, clarify, and define the agenda. That might mean letting team members know one of the agenda items might hit some nerves. Remind the group of their commitment to learning together and to listening respectfully to the discussion. You are building strategies to look for answers and, understanding the obstruction, chew on it a bit and then let it go and move on.

It's all right to say "I understand it's not something you'd choose to deal with or do, but it's where we are right now so let's work on this together" or "This isn't something we all relish; however, I think we can find a way to make this work if we put our minds to it" or "Let's have a whine/wine night soon as a team, then we really have to let this one go and move on."

Conversations around teaching and learning to strengthen the group's practices are a professional responsibility, so plan how time will be used, think through the possible pitfalls ahead of time, and be confident that after rich and full discussions, solutions will emerge.

Is there a structure for addressing controversial or heated issues that can be used? Is there a protocol in place for making decisions that have majority support? Yes, many are available online, so Google problem-solving models and find one that works for your leadership style. You'll find almost all contain these basics in one form or another:

- identify the issue or problem specifically;
- list the pros and cons;
- identify the barriers;
- allow all to voice their opinion;
- do not pose a solution too soon or stop the process;
- ensure everyone speaks once before any second turns are taken;
- allow think time to process the options;
- find points of agreement; and
- fashion a solution and develop an action plan.

As teacher leader, have a strategy to open and close the meeting, set time limits, and share your goal for the discussion: "today I'd like us to really take this issue apart to see where we have areas of agreement and areas to refine. Let's agree that by 4 PM, we'll take what we have and use this as our starting point on Wednesday if we haven't found a solution."

Use data when you have it so that dialog is grounded. Take every opportunity to stay on target; the group is a teaching and learning team, and what you ultimately do must be good for students and their learning.

As the group's leader, it is important to recognize emotions for what they are and acknowledge them. That doesn't mean you agree with the emotion or how it was expressed, but it does show you heard it. Most teams don't reach 100 percent agreement on everything they do. However, learning to disagree, to risk discomfort, to share insights and feelings and work through these together, patiently, helps the team become more productive as a result.

As teacher leader, stay centered on your purpose and check in to see that you are listening to what's said and what's not said; check body language.

There is a time to call a halt and take five, breathe deeply and set the topic aside for another time if need be. Use this sparingly but you'll know when it feels right. Then, when you do return to the issue, define the salient points and ask the group to come at it in a different way.

Leaders who confidently frame these conversations are putting their leadership into action, so be patient, be focused, and keep it civil. You are modeling what you expect: civil and respectful problem solving. You know others are watching so show how it's done!

LOST CONTROL

Dear Jan: Our team spends 90 percent of our time gossiping, complaining about students, or rehashing the weekend sports. Even as the leader, I don't seem to have any control of all this. Am I supposed to just bear it or work around the team? What are my options?

Leading a group of adult peers is hard work even for those with organizational, management, and human relations skills. As Chen and Rybak (2004) point out, "Leadership is not about having the answers. It is not as much about being in charge as it is about enabling the group to reach its goals" (p. 30).

The dynamics of leading teams of adults who are often outspoken and who value their time and their way of doing things can cause even the most effective teacher to get weak in the knees. Add to that the reality that some teacher leaders were selected for the position without the training, background, or support that would help them to be effective. What you are describing isn't unheard of. There is a body of knowledge and a set of skills that can help leaders develop and more effectively facilitate a peer group.

As with the answer to many of these questions, it begins with a clear sense of purpose and a commitment to work and learn together. Everyone is committed to strengthening teaching and learning together because your students' academic success is everyone's responsibility. Systems are explicit and in place, allowing the various groups to move forward together with an eye on the target, doing whatever it takes to do it well.

Learning organizations don't rest on their laurels; they know they must be positioned to change practices as times and circumstances dictate.

Here's what we know about human dynamics and change. Doug Reeves (2009, February), an educational consultant, looks at change this way, "Leaders of any change know that the dynamics of change calls for strong relationships, a clear focus, sharing of expertise and allowing talented people to move together as a team to support new learning or a new approach."

To effect a change in this group of adults, one that leads away from bantering to conversations that are substantive and introspective, you or a colleague must take ownership of how the group is operating and step up and refocus the group. In essence, build more professional relationships, ones that focus on the purpose of the team.

This can be done gently and with humor.

- You might say, "We're spending lots of this valuable team time complaining and talking about things we can't control . . . like why the quarterback made such a stupid call. I'm going to suggest we

have a whine night or pity party after work soon to continue this conversation. But today, can we refocus? We have a couple of curricular issues to resolve (or instructional strategy to refine, etc.) before I face my fourth period class tomorrow."
- Similarly, you might say, "We've sure picked that bone dry, can we get back to working on X so I can face Mr. Y when he comes to observe me on Friday?"

Before you bail out on this team, if you and others notice that you've lost control or meetings continue to be hijacked, it might be time to find support from a trusted colleague, another teacher leader, the counselor, or the administration.

- You might say "In our team meetings, I'm noticing X and Y dominate all the conversations even when I provide an agenda and the meetings quickly lose focus: can you help? I know some of the challenges in leading this group but I need some meeting pointers? Do you have suggestions?"
- Another approach is saying, "I'm uncomfortable with the tone and direction of the recent meetings. Are there ways I can support you and keep meetings on track? I'm serious about the work we are supposed to be doing. I can come with ideas, suggestions, or a model we can then all critique, but I'd rather we work together so we all have ownership in whatever direction we decide. What do we need to agree to so this is our way of operation?"
- "Gosh, X and Y, that's the second time in this meeting you've been rude to A. It's really hard to sit here and listen to that when we are supposed to be working together. I'm sorry but we have to do better than this."

It might be necessary, in the short run, to talk with one or more of the team members privately if their behavior continues to undermine or sabotage the effectiveness of the group. As difficult as it might be, if one or more teachers continues to ride roughshod over the meeting, you need to call them on that behavior.

It's a risk, but when you consider either working around the team or working to strengthen the team, you do have a choice.

What's missing in your scenario is a sense of joint ownership for learning as a group of professionals and a leader who might need support in building the skills to lead peers. It might take a more concerted focus from all of you to make a difference in the long run and to change the team's conversations. Be clear about what you are about as a team, find ways to build relationships and identify strengths that the team can share to make your work together productive. It's important to stay hopeful and positive; change is hard, but it can be done with persistence and a bit of foresight.

The dignity of each individual is important when you are building capacity for change and growth. Ultimately, it is about building a network of committed individuals around teaching and learning. Leadership is about working with all kinds of people, finding strengths, valuing everyone's contributions, and when necessary, reminding the team about how sacred time is to the work of the group and keeping on target. That shows respect to team members and to your purpose.

Need help with structures for problem solving or running effective and efficient meetings? Check out the Team Initiated Problem-Solving Model from the University of Oregon. The TIP II model is a wonderful visual that is particularly useful. The materials available from the PBIS network are worth investigating and will make a difference.

SAME OLD, SAME OLD

Dear Jan: Since when does allowing students' unlimited access to computers replace teachers in school? I get that these electronics are engaging and keep kids quiet and looking productive but it's the same teacher who showed films every Friday. He still does that but now he grabs the computer lab every Friday afternoon and reads the papers while he says kids are doing makeup work. As teacher leader, how do I let him know I'm on to him?

Your letter has so many layers to it: your role as teacher leader, effective teaching and approaches, use of resources, and when to ask the administrator for professional help with a peer. It is frustrating to know that some people aren't living up to your standards. However, as teacher leader, there are limits to what you can do.

First and foremost, in your role as leader you start with relationships. Do you have a relationship with this teacher so that approaching him to express your frustration is possible without putting either of you in an adversarial position? Does your team talk about expectations for teacher behavior in the computer lab for supervision as well as expectations for students in the lab? If not, can you start that team conversation soon?

Enlist your library/media specialist in this conversation if possible as they've seen it all and can share stories without naming names. This might get the group moving in a position direction with some levity as well. Then there is no finger pointing.

There are several approaches that center on the team's ability to dissect teaching and learning approaches together and align curriculum. These conversations steer clear of personalities but give guidelines to teaching and learning expectations and each teacher's role and set of responsibilities in these areas.

One scenario is to have a team conversation about the uses of technology as tools to support learning; about what is not an appropriate use of these devices; about who is using which tools, applications, and resources; and about how the technology supports class learning goals. As university professor and author Brenda A. Dyak wrote, "Web 2.0 tools . . . have the potential to turn on the learning lights for a generation of digital learners" (2010, p. 38).

When educators leverage technology intentionally and appropriately by integrating tools and applications with instruction to enhance learning, engagement and motivation soar. The key is educators who are content experts who are also familiar with and able to assess which educational tools, applications, programs, devices, and hardware will add value to the particular learning experience. When technology is embedded into learning, access to the tools is critical and might have to be scheduled into class time, if resources (that computer lab) are limited. This might be the case, so check this idea out with the team.

Scenario number two would be to have your team look at the technology standards and outline together which ones are being met in which content areas and when and how. Since teachers are expected to help students meet technology standards with digital tools and applications by embedding them strategically in instruction to enhance, extend, and differentiate learning, this shared responsibility extends to those who use the computer lab, when and for what purposes.

As you align the standards to the team's various curricula, part of the conversation must extend to how this will be done, when and with what resources. That should be a team-wide discussion. "Teachers must understand the pedagogical implications for practice" (p. 8), Will Richardson (2009) reminds us.

Where do you start if the team focuses on aligning content and technology standards? Check the International Society of Technology Standards website for teacher and student standards as well as their lessons connecting curriculum and technology at www.iste.org.

Then build a curriculum unit crosswalk identifying student/activity/technology with a colleague or team member indicating where you might add a specific technology standard and which tool or application would apply to support or enhance learning the skills and concepts you have in mind.

Just as you incorporated academic content standards into lesson plans, number and add the different technology benchmarks to your current planning. Plan how, where and when to introduce, reinforce, and use the various tools, applications, and devices to support learning. And finally, if you rely on a shared computer lab, set guidelines for who uses it when and for what purposes. Friday makeup time should be rare and shared team-wide.

If all this has already been tackled, then a face-to-face conversation might be warranted. These are not always easy conversations, but they are what teacher leaders can expect to face. As teacher leader, it is not your responsibility to admonish or correct a fellow teacher. Teams who collaborate about instruction often make agreements about shared resources. This is a legitimate team goal. For you to question another teacher's methods without this target in place would be to step over the line into teacher evaluation. Not your bailiwick.

It is appropriate to share concerns about use of resources and to give colleagues honest feedback. Here is how you might approach your colleague:

Ask for some time to share a concern that has come to your attention:

- "Bill, do you have a couple minutes after school to talk? I'm hearing some concern about your use of the computer lab and I wanted to bring this to your attention. I'd like to get your take on this and talk together."

If Bill says, "No problem, let's meet," remind him that, as team leader, you have to keep an eye out for access to resources. What can you two work out to make Friday use available to others?

If Bill says that no one's told him it's a problem and that he got the lab first, try this.

- "As a team, sometimes we have to look for ways to make access to scarce resources and time equitable. This can come to the team for discussion. The bottom line is that no one teacher can have the lab each Friday at the end of the day. We need to figure out how to resolve this. I'd like your thinking to be included, too."

Let the person know this is not a onetime occurrence and that you are seeking perspective. There may be a simple answer. Listen and work for a solution that is reasonable.

If none of these make a difference in his practice, your next option may be to ask a trusted administrator for professional advice. You may need to leave it at that level.

These are never easy conversations, but the rule of thumb is not to let things lie and fester but to be honest and objective, without pointing blame, when talking with a colleague. When hard conversations are necessary, keep student learning and their success front and center. And, ask for help when it's appropriate.

FOUR P'S FOR ORGANIZED LEARNING

Dear Jan: We have a brand new teacher at our grade level. She's asking me every day what to do. I'm the department chair so I know it's up to me to help her. I gave her a great book to help her get started but she leans on me for so much. Suggestions short of team teaching?

These days, with the focus on every child learning and teachers being part of professional teams and learning communities, it's even easier to induct new teachers into the profession and that's what you are being asked to do here. We all started at some point, and isn't it wonderful that help was at hand disguised as a colleague, department chair, mentor, or the teacher next door?

First, understand that someone saw something of promise in this young teacher. Be sure you and the team welcome her and let her know she is not alone. Reiterate that you are all there to answer questions and make sure she and her students are successful.

Beginning teachers can be isolated and that's neither good for them nor for their students. Being part of a team means having others there for support, ideas, encouragement, moral support, teaching and management techniques, insights, and suggestions.

The expectations for a productive, organized teaching environment with clear processes, structures, and expectations empower students and create a sense of order. Costa and Kallick (2009) weigh in to emphasize the importance of creating the conditions for learning.

They write, "A nurturing culture is one that is open to ideas and possibilities, but not in the sense of 'anything goes.' The role the teacher takes on is crucial. Teachers must still be in charge and take responsibility for the quality of curriculum delivery and for providing a physically and emotionally safe and disciplined work environment; but they must do so more as a collegial facilitator than as an autocratic dictator. Teachers need to be *doing with* students rather than *dealing to* them" (pp. 19–20). This applies as well to that novice teacher to mentor teacher relationship!

Welcome her questions, ask what she feels is working and where you can be helpful. If it makes sense to you both to meet at a particular time each day for the first two weeks, offer to do that. If meeting with another teacher who also teaches her level or subject is an option, introduce the two. But don't assume that with an introduction, the assistance this teacher needs will be there. Follow up; check in to see what else she might need.

Eventually, you may be able to ease into biweekly or weekly meetings. You are right; you can't take over and do her planning and teaching for her but you can help her talk about what's working and what isn't. Brainstorm what she might do differently, and offer to share the planning guide or system you use. Those are good starts.

As you listen, don't jump ahead and formulate answers and suggestions; give her time to express her thoughts or frustrations and then pose questions like "What might happen if you tried X?" or "How might you take what you did yesterday and tweak it a bit?"

Again, with all your experience and skill, you can help this new teacher build a workable framework for analyzing her management systems, and you can help her look at how she plans for successful student engagement in learning.

Plus, as team leader, you can share what processes or systems are common and agreed upon and used across the team, like where schedules and weekly or monthly calendars are posted, where operational expectations are listed, where learning targets, assignments, and the day's activities are on view. Students know what they will be doing with their time each period from beginning to the end and what materials will be needed and will be ready to learn when the teacher gives his or her signal.

There is efficiency to the order within any given structure as students work in productive and purposeful ways when expectations are clearly communicated. Process, procedures, protocols, and systems are known, named, demonstrated, practiced, and expected so the community of learners functions as a unit. For example,

- "Here's what we do during check-in time, step one . . . step two . . . ;"
- "Here's how we work in small groups"; and
- "Here's how I'll close the learning time each day."

Make each routine or expectation clear; teach it, model it, name it, practice it, expect it, post it, share it, then find opportunities to celebrate when it happens.

The expectations for behavior, the physical organization of the room or learning space, and the systems and processes should all support active, engaged learning and teach students to become self-directed and responsible members of the learning community.

Gregory and Chapman (2002) talk about management in this way, "It is better to prethink management strategies then to have things go 'off the rails' and thus waste valuable learning time while you rethink logistics" (p. 113).

THE FOUR P'S

To establish a sustainable, productive learning environment where teachers and students work together, work with these four ideas, the Four P's for Organized Learning, Tool 3.2 in the appendix. They are:

- Create an operational structure consistent for both teachers and students where both are expected to assume responsibility for the environment. [Predictable]
- Plan intentionally so consistency, processes, and structures support meaningful cognitive engagement. [Purposeful]
- Maintain a learning environment that is creative, inviting, safe, well organized, and student centered. [Productive]
- Establish a culture where relationships and high expectations exist between teachers and students. [Personal]

> **Learning Communities**
> Predictable
> Purposeful
> Productive
> Personal

Here's a look at each of the four.

Predictable

"Classrooms in which there is enough flexibility to reach out to students with varied needs are paradoxical in that they derive much of their flexibility from routine. In fact, clear and predictable classroom routines are probably the difference between productivity and chaos for classrooms where teachers attempt to use variations among learners" (Tomlinson, 2003, p. 47).

Organizing and managing a learning classroom might seem overwhelming for those new to the profession. To keep the focus on students and learning does not mean throwing rules, expectations, and procedures out the window. It means *creating* and *teaching* routines that become part of the culture. Structures foster a sense of safety that supports teaching and learning.

A predictable learning environment allows teachers to teach and students to learn without becoming mired in the daily disruptions that throw routines of managing a classroom into chaos. Make the physical layout work for learning. Configure tables and chairs such that they accommodate the variety of activities you use routinely. Establish quiet spaces, social space, and space for supplies and resources and teach how and when each is available for students.

- List the expectations for working in the classroom or with a resource or when needing help.
- Develop resources and procedures to help students who were absent re-enter the classroom equipped with the learning knowledge they need to participate.
- Arrange the day's or week's agenda, papers, or materials in a designated place and teach students to check for them whenever they come into the room.
- Regularly post as much information as you can: class operating rules, procedure or processes, forms, materials, assignments or information, or timelines or activity schedules; note any major deviations boldly.

- Think through the nonteaching tasks such as distributing papers, taking attendance, and answering process or procedure questions and find ways for students to assume responsibility for these tasks.

In essence, design systems that guide student movement from the time they enter the classrooms until they leave. These processes and routines should support students' ability to use time, space, materials, and each other for learning.

Purposeful

Purposeful lesson planning is a critical component for success in any classroom. As author and researcher Doug Lemov wisely points out,

> Great lessons begin with planning, and specifically with effective unit planning: planning a sequence of objectives, one or possibly two for each lesson, over an extended period of time (say, six weeks). Unit planning means methodically asking how one day's lesson builds off the previous day's, prepares for the next day's and how these three fit into a larger sequence of objectives that lead to mastery. (2010, p. 59)

When planning with the end in mind, a teacher knows where her students are headed and can design activities, strategies, processes, and products that will help them reach the targets. This is often the most difficult undertaking for beginning teachers as they might not be sure where a lesson or unit is headed. Here is where a mentor is critical. Consider these questions together:

- What are you teaching and why?
- How will it be organized?
- Who will do what?
- How will students be involved and supported?
- How will students be grouped for learning?
- Will students have a voice and a choice in any processes or products?
- What teacher roles will you take?
- How will content be taught?
- How will students be taught differently?
- What kinds of resources are needed?
- What support do you need at this point in time?

A beginning teacher or one new to the team might need the support of a mentor to look at what the questions really say about designing a set of lessons or unit of study. With the support of district curriculum and standards guidelines, lesson planning becomes a key ingredient for purpose, productive learning.

Would it be helpful to sit side by side with a beginning teacher and walk through lesson and unit design together? What are the target learning goals? What activities would support these goals? How will the teacher open the lesson; what are the middle and ending components for the first day, the second, and the next? How will the teacher know if students are moving toward that target?

As with any support, follow up. Ask how and what happened or didn't happen and "tell me about"; stay connected as learning occurs with practice. Remember feedback is only helpful if it is goal related, specific, timely, and personalized, to which a caveat must be noted: do not overwhelm this novice with helpful "advice."

Planning together is one way to approach this critical teaching task. Modeling how you approach planning in a step-by-step manner by thinking aloud can be an important teaching moment. Step back into those first years of teaching and share ways to break a quarter's or trimester's worth of objectives into manageable units; identify the targets and find activities that will take students forward. Finally, know when to fade away into the background as the beginning teacher gains confidence and skill.

Productive

When students are engaged in productive learning, the teacher is freed up to assist, conference, reteach, assess, and engage individuals or small groups without having to stop and manage the group. There is an industriousness that stands out.

For this to occur on a regular basis, shift as much of the responsibility for managing the classroom to students by teaching them these types of things so they use their time purposefully:

- where and how to access information they need for the day;
- where and how they enter and leave the learning environment and how they are expected to assume responsibility for their own behavior when in engaged in learning;
- how they will work within the confines of the learning environment;
- how to manage the systems in the classroom: from taking the roll to coming up to speed after an absence;
- how to use tools to help them learn and to track their learning ;
- how to use the physical space for learning;
- how to solve learning problems, from finding resources to asking for help;
- how and where to turn in work or to find work that has been assessed; and
- how to use daily, weekly, and monthly calendar so they know what will happen each day, when the assessment dates are, when work

will be completed, what exemplary work looks like, and why that matters.

Establish clear guidelines for working individually, in small groups, or across teams so everyone knows the rules and understands the expectation for learning in each environment. Practice with students on how to work together productively and talk with them about the outcomes, both for learning, and for operating successfully as a group when established processes and procedures work well.

Expect students to follow through once they are skilled enough to meet the expectations. On occasion, when the hum settles over the room, tell students to stop, look, and listen so they, too, can identify what a productive classroom looks and feels like, then expect it to happen regularly.

Personal

Relationships that are built to support and sustain high levels of intellectual engagement establish rules of civil behavior and an expectation that everyone is part of this community. In this environment, students learn how to treat each other in supportive ways. Put-downs or bullying are not tolerated. It is understood that students need to feel emotionally and intellectually safe to explore and expand their learning potential. Keep rules, expectations, procedures, and consequences clear and simple.

In working with this new teacher, help her be sure students understand why they are in school and what their roles are. They must know how and when to use their voices in ways that are productive and appropriate. Model high expectations for respect by learning each student's name, how each learns best, and what matters to them. When you know students, you are better able to frame learning experiences that meet each one's needs in genuine ways. Engaging with students in a personal way does not mean that teacher and student are equals and friends; it does mean the teacher knows who the student is and uses that information in ways that personalize learning.

Organizing for learning using the Four P's as a framework diminishes the chances of chaos. Every teacher has a responsibility to build and sustain an atmosphere that allows learning to soar. With processes and structures in place that are understood and used with fidelity, the ebb and flow of learning is enhanced.

In dynamic learning communities, colleagues share what is working, how they make it known, how it's supported by students, and what is common and can be instituted across disciplines and classrooms so that what is expected by one is supported by all. A cardinal rule for productive learning across the team!

As new teachers enter the profession, the veteran and more experienced teachers have an obligation to welcome that new member to the team and help that person be successful. It starts with an environment organized and focused on learning. As the teacher leader, when the Four Ps are in place, the chances for engaged learning increase while off-task behaviors diminish. That's what to teach your young colleague. Being her mentor allows you to reflect on your practice as you engage her in learning conversations.

When all is said and done, what's the litmus test? It's having a substitute teacher comment about how productive the class is when you are gone. When the Four Ps are institutionalized, your absence does not hinder classroom operations and students' ability to learn.

CONVERSATION STARTERS

1. What are your team's core values? Are they explicit and known by all? Is that important? Are you comfortable leading the team through the core values protocol? If not, who might come in to help facilitate that? What qualms do you have about doing this?
2. Leading adults is hard work, whatever your leadership style. What disagreements or dilemmas have you faced that challenged your skills? What strategies do you use to address issues? Who do you go to for support when faced with challenges and dilemmas? What skills do you need to help your team move forward?
3. Investigate the many protocols and conversation aids available from the National School Reform Faculty, Harmony Center website, www.nsrfharmony.com, for strategies to engage all team members in deep conversations about teaching and learning. Here are a few particularly helpful to teacher leaders and teams: Looking at Student Work Protocol, Facilitating Learning, and Professional Learning Survey Protocol. Be sure to consult the website for the latest set of materials as many protocols are being updated early in 2014.
4. What strategies or structures do you have in place so that you can defuse problem issues and work together productively? Investigate the TIPS problem-solving model and action-planning materials; take them to the group and see if these materials would allow your work to be more focused, effective and efficient. http://www.pbisnetworking.org.
5. Using the Four P's as a construct, design a system that helps your team provide consistent alignment across classrooms. What will that look like? How can you bring everyone into that conversation?

ADDITIONAL INFORMATION ON DYNAMICS AND LEADING TEAMS

- Charlotte Danielson's article in *Educational Leadership*, 2009, 67(2), beginning on p. 161 "Developing School Leaders" is an informative read.
- "Teacher Leadership: an Assessment Framework for an Emerging Area of Professional Practice," available at http://www.ets.org/Media/Reserach/pdf?RR-10–27.pdf is definitely worth perusing.
- *Thinking at Every Desk* by Derek Cabrera and Laura Colosi is a very practical and insightful book highlighting the skills students need to work globally in the twenty-first-century—a useful book study for teachers and teams.

FOUR

The Focus on Practice

Effective teacher leaders strengthen professional relationships and build the team's collective capacity by focusing on teaching and learning for student success.

COMMUNITIES OF PRACTICE

Dear Jan: I think that when people work together, sharing what they do well in their classrooms and how they do it benefits everyone. I want to spend more of our team time engaging team members in studying and implementing research-based best practices, but it's a shift for our team. What should this look like?

Effective teacher leaders understand that to build a sustainable school model, learning is as important a component for the adults as it is for students. Your goal is to transform your team into "a community of practice." This is done by building meaningful personal and professional relationships to establish a working environment that draws all teachers to the team table for conversations about your teaching practices.

As teacher leader, your role is to move the conversations beyond the day-to-day student management or administrative details to what will make your work as teachers and as professionals more effective. That means talking about teaching strategies, activities, pedagogy, new and emerging practices and trends, and tools and devices; gathering and analyzing formative and summative data; discussing what's working, what's not, and how we can learn together to strengthen all our practices.

Start with a simple conversation designed to determine team members' thinking about teams and how learning together fits into their professional practice. Share how you see that the team working together would strengthen all of your professional practices. Let the group know this is your leadership goal and direction and that you are interested in their reactions and vision to shape your professional learning model.

Talk about communities of practice and define what those professional responsibilities look like. Listen to reactions, consider workable formats, identify the barriers, time constraints, and concerns that this discussion brings up, as they surface. Think about these questions as you move forward:

- Are team members ready to open up with each other and talk about teaching practices they use or might be interested in using?
- What instruction, curriculum, or assessment practices do we already share? Can any of them be our starting point?
- Are any team members already working closely together with curriculum and instruction and is that work being readily shared? How did that collaboration come about and how has that changed practice?
- What problems are we encountering with student learning? What does the data say? How will we tackle those issues together? What might that look like?

As teacher leader, you might be asked how the idea of communities of practice came about. Here's a perspective. Lawyers, doctors, electricians, plumbers, and others have craft knowledge they use along with book learning to meld theory and practice over time to increase their competence and confidence. What these professions have in common as they develop their community of practice is that no one goes to school and then jumps into the profession without expert support.

Support comes from examining case studies, sharing problems, and posing solutions together and from observing each other implementing the solutions with a round of critiquing that follows or watching videos and analyzing them together with an eye toward future implementation.

Apprenticeships and residencies are common examples. These can extend for several years before the practitioner operates solo. This professional sharing of knowledge and skills is focused on strengthening the practices of all practitioners so each client gets the best professional service.

As educational professionals looked for ways to strengthen teaching and learning practices to meet the needs of all students, ones who are diverse and bring a variety of challenges to the classroom, a variety of professional development practices emerged that worked. You might bring one or two of these practices to the attention of your team and consider the pros and cons of each as you look at what you might be able to do together.

Researcher and author Tony Wagner writes about one well-developed model, known as the "lesson study" process, of teacher collaboration to improve practice. Lesson study groups are organized by grade level or subject-content area. These teams meet regularly to discuss the learning challenges of their students and to collaboratively develop lessons that more effectively meet their students' needs.

Using protocols to help organize and document their approach, teachers take turns teaching these model lessons and critiquing one another's work until they feel the lessons are polished enough to share with colleagues. They then use these lessons and feedback in their classrooms, reporting back and dissecting together what works and where changes are needed.

"Critical Friends," developed by the National School Reform Faculty, is one way to approach the lesson study model. Protocols and training are available to any interested group by accessing www.nsrfharmony.org.

An emerging model that supports the "community of practice" ideal is the university–public schools partnership. In this partnership the university provides support for first-year teachers in schools, much like a two-year practicum or first-year residency does. This model is worth investigating if you have a teaching college or university nearby. If you can develop an ongoing dialog with professors about preparing teachers for today's classrooms and offering your school's or team's classrooms for visits and observations, you begin to build for ongoing inquiry.

Is there a model for a "community of practice" that works best? There are many versions from simple dyads, or teaching partners, to team teaching within subject areas, to teams who regularly work in interdisciplinary groups across disciplines with a common group of students.

So what's right for you and your team? All models require the investigation and integration of research and practice, observations and reflection, the use of selected, highly skilled mentor teachers, and a commitment on the part of the entire team to work together. The constants found in any dynamic learning community are:

- Focused leadership;
- Time held sacred for learning conversations;
- Protocols or strategies known to the group to support the work;
- Commitment on the part of all team members to the work; and
- Fidelity to doing the work and follow-through together.

The important point is to define your goals or vision and get commitment from the team. When teachers on teams learn to take an active role in group inquiry, it is possible to take risks and talk about professional improvement.

As you and your team develop your version of the community of practice model, identify one problem, dilemma, or practice to investigate. If warranted, find out if there is an instructional facilitator or subject-area specialist available to be part of your learning team.

Here's how you could begin your community of practice. Identify areas for potential study. Give that list to the team and find one topic all agree to begin studying. Study might begin with reading about a jigsaw activity about a new strategy from a professional research journal. At the conclusion of the activity, survey the team and see if an emerging practice is worth further investigation.

Perhaps the team wants to analyze a set of recent student test scores and decides to disaggregate the data and figure out what the data means with regard to what was learned well and what areas need a boost. At the very least, have DVDs of best practices available for you and the team to use.

When you move into professional conversations about any individual's practices, as the leader do remember teachers are reluctant to brag about or spotlight what they do well, and conversely, are less likely to ask for help when facing a dilemma in their teaching. This hesitancy on team members' parts is natural. You'll need to find ways to make it safe for everyone to ask questions, to risk sharing, and to learn together.

The Case Study Protocol example, Tool 4.1 in the appendix, or a similar tool, can be used as a safe model to begin your group inquiry and assist your team's efforts at collaboration. Then you can adjust or refine how you work together once you get started. It's always advisable to try something new and ask for critical feedback about the process at the end so together you can refine your approach.

As teacher leader, if you set the standard that the team's meetings are about instruction and effective practice, you ground the team's work, one that is focused on sustaining professional learning. Your leadership here will be critical. Take the time to involve your team in this conversation and ask for their help in designing a model that's just right for you and your local circumstances. That's the beauty of teamwork!

DEFINING TEACHING AND LEARNING

Dear Jan: Got a concise definition of teaching and learning our team can use? I think having a clear, common understanding of the two will help us as we look at what we do in the classrooms and what we expect the students to do. Right now, we're all over the map.

It's an interesting, thought-provoking question that has entire schools of thought and theory and years of intellectual study given to doing just that. What does "we're all over the map" mean and can that be good or is it bad? The discussion among your team members about what comprises teaching and the same about learning is a good one to have, if only to illuminate the complexity of both.

So before giving an example of teaching and learning, explore these two terms with the team. What is teaching? How do each of us define it?

How do we know that what we think we are teaching is actually what is taught? The same with learning. Is requiring memorizing teaching? Is teaching more than delivering content?

Now consider the thinking of two well-respected educational teachers/researchers/authors. Use the italicized sentence below with your team and the two quotes that follow to get the conversation started.

It is incumbent on teachers to create the conditions that energize and facilitate learning.

- David Perkins, educator and researcher at Harvard University's Project Zero, explains, "Teaching more paradigmatically involves some pattern of serious interaction beyond delivery. The aim is to emphasize the breadth of the teaching role—not just a matter of providing information and beyond that not just giving assignments and monitoring performance and providing nourishing feedback, but instilling inspiration, provoking inquiry, helping learners to connect up with one another in generative ways, even organizing the classroom or more broadly the learning space so that it is supportive of learning" (personal communication, August, 22, 2010).
- Peter Cookson (2009), educator and author, writes about learning in this way: "Think of learning as a continuum of cognitive and expressive experiences that range from gathering data to the purpose of understanding the world; to organize data into useful and coherent informational patterns; to applying information to real questions and problems and, in the process, creating knowledge; to develop wisdom that offers the hope of transcendent unity" (p. 8).

These are great intellectual discussions that can be carried on for many meetings when you might be looking a more common understanding for the two terms that would help the teams see if the practices each uses activates various levels of thinking and understanding.

It does help to operationalize the definitions of teaching and learning as you work toward a common understanding of the two concepts understood by everyone on the team. Teaching and learning are both dynamic, energetic endeavors; having working definitions helps teachers determine whether or not the chosen practice or strategy *activates* learning.

What follows is one definition for teaching along with some examples of teacher decisions that support student learning:

Teaching is creating the conditions for students to learn.

- Match instruction to target student outcomes.
- Match activity to intended outcome.
- Use ongoing formative assessment to see if students are learning.
- Reteach or adjust instruction based on data collected.
- Teach skills when needed and at the level students need.

- Personalize learning for all students.
- Match social groupings to student need.
- Help student build complexity in their learning.
- Make learning as authentic as possible.
- Establish systems for intervention, acceleration, and classroom management.

How do you know that what was taught and what you intended to teach was what students learned? A definition for learning follows, along with examples of how students demonstrate what they have learned.

Learning is evident when students are able to use or reshape the skills, knowledge, or concepts they have been taught. Here are some examples.

- Defend a thesis stating a principle based on information gathered in a study.
- Identify a problem and propose solutions to solving the problem.
- Argue, debate, or defend a personal position based on a content study.
- Build or design a new product or structure based on a content study.
- Keep a journal where progress or lack of progress is cited and actions taken are recorded.
- Identify different perspectives or biases. Explain reasons for differences.
- Talk about content and what was learned in a free and open discussion.
- Pass a formal assessment.
- Engage in conversation with a content expert.

Why does having definitions of teaching and learning matter?

When teachers know what they want to teach and what they want students to learn, it's easier to identify the steps and processes and match approaches needed to ensure students actually learn what was intended. Teachers create the conditions that energize and facilitate learning.

That means teachers must know what they are teaching, and match the skills, concepts, ideas, and questions they want students to be able to use to strategies and approaches that will give students ways to enter into the content. When goals are identified and the level of learning is targeted, giving students the resources and a roadmap helps frame their work. It's all very intentional from the beginning.

Beyond a dialog of definitions, what you as teacher leader can do is help operationalize the two. Find a device or model to focus your teaching/learning dialog and identify concrete actions that educators do that are attributes of teaching and learning.

Consider what a group of teachers in the Charlotte-Mecklenburg School District in North Carolina did with Marzano's taxonomy; see Tool

4.2 in the appendix for an example of a device that helps pinpoint levels of learning and was used as a tool for teacher dialog.

Your team might want to take this taxonomy of thinking, consider its framework, and develop a model like it to use across teams or disciplines. This approach is an effective starting point to identify what level of learning and understanding is expected in an activity or unit of study beyond any one classroom. The point is to move the conversation forward, not just admire the conversation.

As the team's leader, offer one of your units of study and ask team members if they can identify elements of your teaching and learning definitions and if they can find the match between those elements and the unit of study. Did having the two definitions make a difference in actual day-to-day practice? What did you expect? Why is this important?

These conversations are a good example of team inquiry and can lead to dynamic discussions because they center on what happens in the classroom. For learning to occur, the material must be taken in and actively processed, connecting what is known to new knowledge or information that is then used in a new way. That's the definition of learning and what you want happening in all the team's classrooms. Robust conversation and an action plan should follow!

A PLACE FOR STANDARDS

Dear Jan: We continue to debate the issue of standards and some of us wish the Common Core State Standards would go away. We don't have much time to work together on them; in fact we have other more pressing issues to deal with. However, knowing that's wishful thinking, can you help our team use these standards?

Start by understanding standards for what they are. "The Common Core State Standards provide a consistent, clear understanding of what students are expected to learn, so teachers and parents know what they need to do to help them. The standards are designed to be robust and relevant to the real world, reflecting the knowledge and skills that our young people need for success in college and careers" (Common Core State Standards Initiative website, http://www.corestandards.org).

Standards identify the essential skills and knowledge teachers are to teach and students are to learn in each discipline by grade level. It is the school district's responsibility to develop a rigorous curriculum where content, concepts, skills, and assessment tasks are tied to those standards.

Traditionally, students who study the content and pass the tests in which standards are embedded are deemed successful learners. Knowing and mastering discrete facts and recalling bits of content information are no longer the sole learning goal. Standards are a starting point when it is understood that the purpose of schools, more than socializing, sorting, or providing order, is learning.

Your question is timely; it indicates that your team is ready to take the next steps to make learning robust and engaging and be standards based.

As the teacher leader, you might engage your team with these questions about your current work with standards.

- What standards are you expected to teach over the course of the year?
- Where is there an overlap between or among content areas?
- Who is currently teaching which standards?
- If a standard is included in several disciplines, who will be responsible for teaching which standard?
- What are the best practices for teaching to various standards?
- What learning tasks will students be asked to do?
- How will information be given to students about how to work and how to meet the standard?
- What materials and resources are available to use so we aren't reinventing the wheel and can get right into standards-based teaching and learning projects?

As teaching and learning decisions are being made, have teachers match curriculum content with strategies and approaches that optimize learning. Post which standards students are working toward so students know specifically what is expected of them before they are asked to complete any work. Communicating the criteria for success is an essential first step in framing any learning experience for students.

To make working with standards more than simply checking off boxes, transition from memorization of facts to a practice that is more conceptual, exploratory, in-depth, meaningful, and personal. When core standards are embedded in units of study that are designed around key concepts and relevant big ideas, you build in opportunities for high cognitive engagement.

These days, successful students must be able to filter volumes of information, have the thinking capabilities to distinguish that which is relevant from that which is not, and be able to defend their decisions with solid reasoning. As you guide the team, make working with complex ideas, patterns, trends, and finding critical connections the academic focus. Use the core standards and all the relevant material available on the www.corestandards.org website to guide the way.

You are right; these rich standards are not going away, nor should they. As teacher leader, show that you value these standards and find ways to weave your work around them, continue to prioritize finding and sharing the many rich resource materials available that support the standards, and ask the team to give time and thoughtful attention to the standards.

Knowing that an implementation cycle isn't established until three years of focus and work to refine a practice are in place, do all you can to define your team's work around effective teaching and learning, using standards as the base. It will pay off but it won't happen overnight. That's easier said than done, but that's the essence of teacher leadership; define the focus and negotiate everything else.

WHICH BEST PRACTICES?

Dear Jan: Do you have a list of instructional strategies that are deemed best practice that I can bring to the department? I know there are lots of options; I'm just not sure which are best and which would work for us.

A best practice is defined broadly as a method or technique that has consistently shown results superior to those achieved with other means, and that method or technique is used as a benchmark. In your case, a best practice is one where instructional approach or strategy matches student learning needs so target goals can be reached. Using this approach guarantees the same results regardless of the student population.

Your question tells me that either your team is ready to learn something new or different together, to engage in professional learning, or the traditional "teacher as expert" approach has been the team's modus operandi and it is now time to push forward.

An example of one model you might use to jumpstart a team conversation is the New Learning Environments chart, Tool 4.3 in the appendix, that comes from the National Educational Technology Standards for Students. It is prefaced with "Traditional educational practices no longer provide students with all the necessary skills for economic survival in today's workplace. Students today must apply strategies for solving problems using appropriate tools for learning, collaborating, and communication. The following chart lists characteristics representing traditional approaches to learning and corresponding strategies associated with new learning environments" (p. 19).

As you and your team consider the two columns in Tool 4.3, what's the reaction? Are you sensing agreement or conflict, questions or strong reactions? Take the time to talk through the continuum of practices that these two sets of end points represent. Remember it isn't either one or the other; it's where on the teaching/learning continuum each teacher is and where changes or shifts are needed to meet the learning needs of students in classrooms today.

Then ask the team to identify which one or two of the practices they are interested in learning more about and which ones might be important for student learning. That's a first step.

You and the team might consider these additional strategies and models of instruction. They fit into your "best practices" question.

- *Teaching for transfer*: providing opportunities for students to apply a problem-solving strategy, for example, to a new situation within the same content area (low level) or teaching the same strategy but providing opportunities to use the same strategy in a new or different context such as a different content area, for example (high level).
- *Metacognitive strategies*: asking students to develop a plan of action for reaching a specific learning goal and then using the mind to monitor progress on the plan and to reflect on progress made and corrections needed.
- *Concept formation*: a conceptual strategy to help students see relationships between groups of things relevant to the concept. The concept is presented to students and a set of attributes is generated by students, or the teacher provides students with the list of attributes for the concept. Then students are given some examples and asked to group like things (common attributes) together and to label each group. The idea is for students to discover the complex nature of the concept.
- *Concept attainment*: a conceptual strategy to help students understand a concept by looking at exemplars and nonexemplars. A list containing both is given to students, and students are asked to group like things together. The students study the list to identify what the exemplars have in common. Naming the concept is the last step.
- *Concept mapping*: a concept map is a graphic representation of a concept. Each important attribute of the content is identified and linked to relations though lines and arrows. Once the concept map is completed, the main attributes have been identified and the relationships between and among attributes have been identified.
- *Compacting*: this is a strategy where students are assessed to see what they might know or be able to do within a course of study. Students then move forward based upon their knowledge, skill, and ability to work more rapidly through the material or to work with more complex materials, for example.
- *Problem-based learning*: students use their knowledge of how to identify and solve problems to work as professionals do in the field when studying a real problem.
- *Independent study*: a course of study designed for a student who is able to work at an accelerated pace or who is extremely knowledgeable or talented in a content area and who needs a different experience from what other students need within a content area, for example.

As the team leader, after sharing the list above and the chart with the group, identify which strategies or practices are already being used and by how many teachers. Ask if any one approach in particular resonates with or intrigues the group. You can then decide which to explore more in-depth.

Follow up by reading about the strategy, finding a podcast or webinar to attend together, asking the district's or school's instructional director for resources, visiting and observing someone using the approach, and conferring with them about where and how they started.

When ready, pair up to design lessons that ensure fidelity of approach when implementing the components of the new strategy. This could be a perfect opportunity to do a peer observation for feedback and support, putting teamwork into action.

As teacher leader, do celebrate each time a new instructional practice is tried, evaluated, refined, and added to your group's repertoire. To keep learning fresh and engaging, it is important to search out new ways of doing things and to acknowledge the work being done along the way. Motivation comes from working persistently and finding some degrees of success.

In this way, you are also adjusting and changing your approach so more students learning styles are engaged. Hold the focus of your work to strengthening practice; negotiate other demands or weave them into this implementation cycle so that change takes hold. That's your role as the teacher leader; show what you are doing and the results that you obtain. It's your best ally.

Keep in mind, best practice applies to any teaching strategy or method that a teacher or team of teachers actually puts into practice that garners the expected results consistently.

TAKING TIME

Dear Jan: It seems we're being asked to hurry up, work smarter and faster, that time is an enemy. I do think that there are times when you must take the time to think, to consider, to ponder, to process everything. Am I wrong here; shouldn't time be a friend, a resource?

Hooray for understanding that not everything is worth rushing through; both adults and students need to learn how to slow down, turn it off, tune in to their inner thoughts, and actually let the mind cool down.

In this fast-paced, multitasking 24/7 world, sometimes it is important to slow the mind down and deliberatively think about only one thing at a time. Deep thinking, making connections, pondering the meaning of a written piece, mentally processing disparate ideas to find a common thread, and allowing ideas to ruminate and creativity to percolate all take uninterrupted, unlimited processing time.

Unfortunately, this seems to be increasingly difficult to do. Perhaps that's all the more reason to make it part of your team's and classrooms' standard operating procedure.

Learning to slow the mind and examine what you are thinking, considering, or pondering is a skill that is rarely taught but is exceedingly important when learning is at stake. Using and fitting time to tasks is a skill that is essential in today's multitasking, how fast can we get it done, world.

What you are really talking about is using metacognition as a tool in your repertoire. As you are probably aware, metacognition means thinking about your own thinking. Some of the characteristics of metacognition are reflection and slowing down and paying attention to what your thought processes are.

Time and space are critical elements. Some people need solitude for this type of deep thinking, others need to time to walk and let their minds wander; still others find that leaving the idea, problem, or issue alone for some time is the best way to allow solutions or ideas to emerge. Finding and taking time to go inside your thinking is actually a very good use of time as a resource. As teacher leader, it is incumbent on you to remind the group of the value of taking time to let ideas percolate, to allow the mind to wander and be creative in approaching dilemmas and circumstances.

When you meet with others, do talk about where you got an insight to some team issue; perhaps it came to you during a walk in the woods that you could create a grid that showed how the six district mandates came together, say, or while waiting for your daughter at music lessons, how the music reminded you of the composition of an orchestra and how that was a great metaphor for the team's part in the school reorganization. Verbalizing your use of time and reflection gives this skill importance.

This stepping away, in essence putting the problem or situation on a back burner for a time, is important for thinking. Getting some distance from thinking, taking a mental break from how one is thinking or what one is experiencing, allows other perspectives to emerge:

- What do others think and say?
- If I did this, what would happen?
- This happened because I did this; what now?
- Is this the best alternative for me?
- What do I need to do differently?
- What mistakes did I make in my thinking?

Stepping away to think about, wrestle with, and reflect gives insights we might otherwise not have about how we work, learn, and communicate. Stopping to monitor ones thinking and the decisions made is metacognition in action.

Many teachers do this automatically as they teach a lesson. When a teacher looks out at the faces in the classroom, she might think, "I'm seeing some confusion. Did I miss anything? Maybe I need to stop and check level of understanding again before I move on." Taking time to think before just moving forward requires a great deal of sophistication. With practice, it becomes a useful tool for both adults and students and is a skill to nurture.

Personal reflection is another skill that is underestimated in importance and uses time as an important resource. When a teacher takes the time to think about his work, to analyze how and why he thinks and feels as he does, to ask questions about why something worked or didn't work and to use that information going forward, that's personal reflection. Reflection provides direction, instills confidence, and uses the "mind's eye" to clarify and crystallize thinking.

In this way, personal reflection supports learning. When teachers reflect about their teaching practices, strengths, and skill, they analyze what worked and what needs fine tuning. When teams of teachers come together to reflect openly about what they need to do to build a team synergy that supports teaching and learning, the practices of all participants grow.

Reflections allow missteps to be acknowledged and lessons learned to be solidified. These insights provide strategies, processes, and avenues that can be used successfully in other endeavors. One example of a process teachers might consider using to begin this critical practice is the self-reflection process described in Tool 4.4 in the appendix.

Making time for thinking, finding the space and opportunity to think deeply, is necessary in this hectic, multispeed world for both students and teachers. Going faster isn't always better; intentionally slowing down can be the most productive use of time. Being deliberate and taking the time to consider, to ponder, to ruminate informs our thinking. It doesn't happen when the mind is distracted by other noise.

Teachers are well advised to give themselves permission and the time to stop and think, to model how this is done and why it matters. As teacher leader, make this a skill you value.

MORE THAN POINT AND CLICK

Dear Jan: Our kids are so far ahead of us with various electronic devices and especially with social media. How do I get the team to ramp up their use of these emerging technologies as well?

Technology and social media are significant parts of many students' lives. You are correct in implying we, as teachers, need to understand that and find ways to harness that interest and embed what is appropriate and timeless into how we teach and find ways in which technology supports learning.

Before you make yourself and your team crazy by trying to learn the latest and greatest new device, remember this: Deftness with devices means one can navigate the tool; it does not mean one can necessarily evaluate its strengths and effectiveness in a particular situation. Students can point and click and maneuver around the surface of many devices, but it is teacher expertise with content and background knowledge and strength in understanding curriculum and concepts that make a tool worth using to support learning.

So while there is no escaping that Web 2.0 tools and applications are part of the personal and educational landscape, just like any new program or practice that comes along, teams must be sure they start with curriculum goals, standards, concepts, and skills and then find tools that work to support and enhance learning.

Once that is firmly understood, time can be spent investigating various ways to use electronics to deliver content and engage students. Traditional practices as well as digital resources can be explored. What works for different students and different teachers is on a wide continuum. Many tools of technology support individual styles and learning needs.

Using technology doesn't mean abandoning traditional approaches, strategies, and methods. It means using the correct tools to enhance and engage students as they build their skills and knowledge so that they are able to continue with that learning without regard to time or place.

A bonus with technology is meeting students where they are and preparing them for the world they are inheriting. It is rich with electronic and digital communication devices. If teachers and teams are to harness students' curiosity and help students learn to persist on increasingly difficult skills and tasks, learning and technology must be "just one way we do business" around here.

Unfortunately, throughout this country, just when teachers need more time for professional development to enhance their own learning (digital and otherwise), funds for education are limited and tight. Teacher leaders, those who have any autonomy for using time as money, should engage their team in conversations about what resources (time, money, expertise) they have and what they can do with them. Priorities must be made to use these resources in ways that support the team's core values and beliefs. It is simply a matter of choice.

Without question, these are often hard choices between what we'd like and what the current reality is. But when a school or team puts a twenty-first-century education for all students as the priority and where resources are spent (technology and dollars for training, for instance) show the level of commitment to fulfilling that vision. It's always a choice—if teaching and learning are the team's priority focus, tools of technology and training to use these appropriately and with fidelity in all instruction are "how we do business."

Kyrene Elementary School, in the Tempe, Arizona, school district, posts this provocative statement on their website. "Our primary focus is not the state-of-the-art technology but how that technology effects the state-of-the-art education of our students." They use their limited dollars to buy time, for staff development training and for studying a variety of best instructional practices aimed at providing all teachers the pedagogy, strategies, and tools that make a difference in how students learn content in their classrooms.

- Does your school/district have a current vision and set of beliefs that blend traditional and emerging practices, or is there a need to revisit them so they better reflect the changing world in which students are being educated?
- Are keeping students in school and increasing the number of those students who reach high school graduation priorities on your school district's radar?

If the answer to those two questions is yes, then learning to use technology to support teaching and learning is an important learning goal for your team of professionals. Maybe someone from the math/science department is a skilled technical writer and is willing to investigate and write a grant to build expertise and integrated learning using STEAM technology. Offer to take a team member's duties so they can write that grant.

Rotary Clubs and local business groups will often give funds in exchange for a service or connection to school projects. Reach out and don't assume "no" means "no." Have students participate in these presentations, using media they have created to support learning, to personalize your requests. Make sure, if you are given money, to let the funding group know how the money was spent and to what end.

Teachers, teams, and departments might take the time allocated for early-release training days and in-service days, add those minutes together and rearrange the schedule by combining separate minutes into blocks. Then schedule blocks of time to engage in training and in deep conversation about teaching, learning, and how to leverage technology. Goals might look like this:

- Align curricula horizontally and vertically, indicating how, where, and when curriculum standards are met.
- Pinpoint where technology standards and expectations will be blended into instruction across and between content areas.
- Investigate a wide variety of tools and applications, defining what each does and where it might enhance or extend learning.

- Decide which tools/applications support what kind of learning; agree who will teach what and to what level of mastery.
- Create common expectations for use of tools and applications and commit to following through with these expectations.
- Hold technology training workshops with others in their school or on their team to take advantage of each other's expertise with various tools and applications.
- Investigate local and national resources that will add to teachers' expertise and ease in infusing instruction with technology, from online workshops to book studies and conferences.

High expectations for all apply to the adults in the school as well as the students. As a teacher leader, carve out team time, intentionally, for professional development around emerging technology that supports teachers' needs, and keep that time for learning sacred.

Find alternative ways to do routine, administrative, or management business using an online communication tool. Model and demonstrate a new device once a month; see if you can generate interest by piquing their curiosity. Hold a drawing for a new gadget or device. Using technology regularly to support teaching and learning just needs to be part of the new way *we work together*.

Even with time, money, and all the support in the world, if some on your team still classify themselves as technophobes, where do you start?

James Leu, a California high school technology teacher, shares this advice:

> Use only tools they feel might benefit their classroom. Most teachers already access grades and test scores online, some do unit or weekly lesson plans online that indicate standards various lessons are designed to meet.
>
> When moving to add technology to instruction, start small, observe a fellow teacher who teaches a similar class and is more attuned to technology to demystify how hard it is to infuse some tool or application into a presentation or assignment. Then investigate Google accounts, see if your school or district has a Google Education account and play around with this tool for sharing ideas and documents with your team, department or a particular class. (personal communication, 2012)

All teachers want their students to learn and achieve. Teachers on the team can start with web-based tools referenced in your textbook at the end of any unit. Ask a teaching partner what he or she uses and have him or her model it for you in your class. Barter one set of talents and skills for someone else's talent with technology as a learning tool. Remember, you are a professional; you must continue learning or you and your students will fall behind.

As teacher leader, put the power of time and training into ongoing professional growth as a team goal, differentiating how time is used to fit the needs of the team. Just as with any new approach, coaching, support, and focused practice are important. Ultimately, it's about curriculum content and the many varied tools that support learning, some of which are electronic and digital.

POWERLESS

Dear Jan: I feel like I'm powerless! With standards and curriculum all decided and the school district telling us what our goals are, where do I have any choice left or autonomy? Several of my colleagues are with me on this. We'd love to know if this is all there is.

As a teacher, you have the power to bring learning to life, to help students see connections, relevance, and meaning. All the magic that happens between students and content lies squarely with you. Making learning irresistible so students want to come to school and work hard and building relationships between students and learning is powerful. You own that!

The mandates and restrictions you mention can feel stymieing; top-down management, imposed standards, and outdated or paced curriculum can lead to poor morale and less than satisfied employees. However, we are each responsible for our own attitude as a starting place. Moving from disenfranchisement to empowerment means finding where you have a voice and choice, which is important to your well-being and to reviving your joy in your chosen profession. It sounds as though that joy might be missing.

Bear in mind that all the standards, pacing guides, bell schedules, and test schedules are organizational structures put in place to assure order and a sense of standardization. Teachers have control and choices within the instructional domain and in personal and professional relationships. Investigate Framing Content, Process and Product Tool, Tool 2.3 found in the appendix, and look for those areas in your control. What you do with your colleagues matters; how you interact with, engage with, and motivate your students matters as well.

In many schools, teacher-led learning teams are given authority to target professional learning to enhance their repertoire of teaching practices and how they will go about implementing practices. These teams can chose to use time flexibly as they negotiate instructional time to meet learning targets or differentiate content between subjects or members of the disciplines.

Even if you aren't one of those lucky team members, teachers as content experts do have choices when designing strategies to use to showcase learning, to organize concepts so that students see connections, and to plan celebrations to recognize learning, such as demonstrations or public showcasing of projects and products.

What happens within your classroom and between and among colleagues that impacts students and learning is a teacher responsibility. How you meld the themes, threads, and major concepts within your curriculum and between or among other departments has a large effect as a powerful motivator on students and their learning. That's in your hands. That's where your joy comes from.

For teachers and many teams, working with the administration and acknowledging that there are areas that are their domain and others that are yours helps give power back to teaching and learning decisions.

Putting power into the hands of the people doing the work has benefits beyond a happy work force. By-products are engaged, motivated, and energized professionals taking responsibility and using all their talents to improve performance!

Finally, a last thought. Some teachers lend their voices to the leadership of their teams and their departments, either informally or in a more formal designation, so they can influence and be part of the decision-making process. Consider whether that might be an avenue you would want to take. Meanwhile, be intentional in your teaching, be strategic in how you voice your dissatisfaction, and know that your joy comes from those relationships with both the adults and students with whom you are in contact daily. Make teaching and learning your focus and see if that brings back your enthusiasm.

Know that so much of what really matters in schools is that the incredible relationship you build between a student and learning is the most powerful and enduring one. That one rests with you.

CONVERSATION STARTERS

1. Are you leading a community of practice? What defines your work? What percentage of the group's time is spent in professional development together? What tells you this is so? Ask the team for feedback around this and pinpoint models to strengthen your work together.
2. Ask each team member to succinctly define teaching and learning. Share those definitions and see what critical elements all of them include. Ask for a couple of examples of the definitions in action and dissect these together. How will this exercise focus the work you each do in your classrooms?
3. Make it a point to read your district's technology curriculum. At what grades and in what subjects do students learn about acceptable, ethical use of web-based resources, copyright policies, online safety, search procedures? Who teaches students to critically analyze sources and sites for accuracy, bias, and truth? When are skills introduced and reinforced? Then check to be sure all your students

have had access to this teaching. Set up fresher mini-lessons as needed.
4. What steps are being taken in your school to assure that teams and teachers have a voice and a choice in teaching and learning? Use the Framing Content, Process, and Product chart, Tool 2.3, as a starting point. Can each member identify examples where the talents and experiences of both formal and informal leaders have furthered the organization's or the team's goals? If not, why not and how can this be rectified?
5. Generate a list of things over which you have control. Are relationships prominent on that list? Is working with your team? How about the joy of learning?

ADDITIONAL INFORMATION ON THE FOCUS ON PRACTICE

- David Conley has a comprehensive article on common core standards in *Educational Leadership's* March 2011 issue called "What Students Need to Learn." Check out his article on pages 16–20.
- *Teach Like a Champion: 49 Techniques That Put Students on the Path to College*, by Doug Lemov, is a book that describes a plethora of techniques in concrete, specific, and actionable ways so teachers, even novices, can implement them immediately. His book comes with a DVD showcasing exemplary teachers using these techniques in thirty-second segments. Perfect for teams to use to spur professional conversations.
- *Leadership Ensemble: Lessons in Collaborative Management from the World's Only Conductorless Orchestra* is the story of the Orpheus Orchestra, a truly leaderless organization. The elements that made them successful apply to schools and teams as well. It's a compelling read.
- National Technology Standards for Students provides teachers, tech planners, and others with frameworks and standards to guide them in establishing enriched learning environments supported by technology. Lessons, activities, and web resources are included here: .
- George Lucas Education Foundation is a nonprofit that documents and disseminates models of the most innovative practices in K–12 schools nationally. The web site contains all multimedia content published since 1997: www.edutopia.org/.
- *Wikis, Podcasts, and Other Powerful Web Tools for Classrooms*, Will Richardson's 2009 instructive and insightful book for educators, is a must read for those who want to get started and aren't sure how. Corwin Press, 2nd edition.

FIVE
Shifts and Change

Effective teacher leaders create the conditions of others' success. They build relationships and engage others in meaningful work around teaching and learning.

JUSTIFYING PROFESSIONAL LEARNING TEAMS

Dear Jan: Everyone says learning team structure is important for teachers, yet we are having to justify our teams and team time to the district for budget reasons. They seem to think this is an expense the district can well afford to drop but we need time working together to meet our professional responsibilities as we're expected to do so many things for so many students and do them well. Are there arguments we can use to help the powers that be understand we need this structure for our learning, too?

Professional learning communities and teams are the organizations—the structures—that link teaching, learning, best practices, and student achievement together in a seamless whole. Effective working teams trust in the collective wisdom, experience, and expertise of all team members to move their work forward. Educators understand that in building a sustainable twenty-first-century model school, learning is as important a component for the adults as it is for students.

Professional collaboration is essential precisely because learning and implementing new practices, strategies, or ways of instruction takes thought and attention and must be intentional. To change and improve takes time, practice, feedback, and adjustments all before any new practice or change becomes institutionalized. Once and done is not the recipe for successful change; research on the effective implementation cycle proves that.

That is the compelling reason for any learning team. And for teams to function well there must be designated time for their professional growth. Period. Nonnegotiable.

For teams to meet during the work day does cost money and is of concern in this age of reduced revenues and tight operating budgets. Since time = $, your strategy must be to equate the team's ongoing professional training to time and money as a viable option for teachers to learn, understand, acquire, and institutionalize the new X (add the change) so that all students can be successful.

The National Commission on Teaching and America's Future conducted extensive research reviews to identify practices that improve teaching effectiveness and student achievement, reported in *Education Week*, June 28, 2010. One significant finding is that a collaborative learning culture helps educators meet the constantly evolving learning needs of their students.

Tom Carroll, president of the National Commission on Teaching and America's Future, along with Hanna Doerr, program manager at the commission, discussed learning teams and the future of teaching. In part they wrote,

> Based on our findings, we have concluded that the nation has a pressing need, and an unprecedented opportunity to improve school performance by using learning teams to systematically induct new teachers into a collaborative learning culture-teams that embed continuous professional development into the day to day fabric of schools that are constantly evolving to meet the needs of 21st century learners. This calls for a cultural shift in schools, a shift that is gaining momentum across the country.

Teams that embed professional development regularly into their time together to build student success:

- listen actively to the ideas of others;
- challenge conventional wisdom if necessary;
- search for alternative ways to present and engage the learner;
- learn together as professionals;
- question one another respectfully;
- seek new knowledge;
- try new strategies;
- let go of outdated or ineffective ideas and practices;
- embrace change. and
- work a little outside of one's own comfort zone.

When teams define their time for focused professional learning, the quality of what happens in every classroom is enhanced. Teacher leaders must be proactive in sharing and communicating the professional learning the team has undertaken and to regularly communicate and link that work to students' success. Highlight data, bring testimonials, demonstrate exemplary work, be strategic, be intentional, and be specific; focus on teaching and learning gains.

Sometimes district folks and the community at large don't know how time is being used. It is incumbent on a teacher leader and the principal's leadership cadre to highlight adults' learning. When the various communities hear what your teams are studying and learning professionally, as you create highly engaged, highly productive learning environments for all your students, time and the value of working together becomes more visible and significant.

In redefining team time as professional-learning time, the role of teacher leader takes on increasing significance. Teacher leaders must model ways that bring differing points of view together, embrace all levels of experience, lead in a nonjudgmental manner, keep lines of communication open, and help the team set professional learning goals focused on student success.

As goals are met and students reap the benefits of this teamwork, evidence and artifacts and demonstrations of learning should be shared across teams and potentially other schools so the benefits of the new or emerging strategies are shared. Allowing others in a school or district to be part of this sharing can only strengthen the model and bring value to the approach.

When time = $, showcasing results is smart business!

You might not be able to pencil out a perfect dollar match by multiplying personnel hourly costs to equate with monies set aside for professional training, but when faced with the benefits of professional growth like this, minds can change. It is a different way of allocating staff development dollars.

See that, when you approach your district and school board as learning partners, you are prepared to offer several options for team meetings. If team time on a daily basis is prohibitive, what about setting aside two hours each week for teams to engage in professional training with an early-release or late-start day? Could half days be scheduled monthly for teams rather than full days for in-service so regular training occurs?

Professional learning is not a one day, before the new school year starts activity. Rather, professional learning requires ample time to engage in study and professional inquiry through the year, with time to discuss strategies and observe each other practicing techniques and sharing feedback. Until that time comes, finding ways to ensure teams use time together well hinges on team relationships and their commitment to focusing on teaching and learning together.

KEY LESSONS

Dear Jan: I am a department leader and our departments seem to have very different understandings of technology standards and practices. What lessons have other districts learned with regard to technology and teaching? I'd like someone else's study to insert into our departments' conversation so we can all be on the same page as we move into the future with technology.

Here are key lessons we have shifted from numerous conversations with technology and innovation directors and teacher leaders across the country. These all support one premise: Technology is a tool to support teaching and learning. The six lessons that follow may be useful in working with your department leaders.

Lesson 1

Technology is one of many tools, activities, strategies, and experiences that engage students and make learning relevant.

Keep in mind learning happens in many places: community gardens, field experiences, nature walks, internships, simulations, attending and participating in civic meetings or court hearings, volunteering at animal shelters and food kitchens, and growing vegetables and selling them at neighborhood markets. Technology and its various applications is another learning opportunity. When learning is connected to content through essential questions and big ideas and is relevant to the lives of the young people involved, technology is only one of many appropriate ways to invite and energize learning.

It's not really about technology; it's about finding a variety of strategies, methods, and activities that advance learning and inspire loving to learn. Technology is just one means to that end.

Lesson 2

Assure access. All students must have opportunities to use technology for learning. These doors must open for all students if we as educators believe technology is a powerful catalyst for learning. If assuring equal access to technology for each and every student is questionable in your school, team, or grade level, then honest, courageous conversations are in order. This may take place in your team, in your department, or with your administrators.

Just as it's inappropriate to ask some students to learn their multiplication tables or to read at grade level but not others, giving some students access to technology and digital citizenship curriculum and telling others to stick to paper and pencil math games is unacceptable. All students need access to high levels of instruction, to be held accountable for the learning goals, and to have equal access to good teaching. Again, teaching is about building capacity and talent as well as knowledge and skills. Access to tools of technology to enhance and deepen learning applies to all students.

Notice these examples didn't say a certain select group of students would be able to engage in these learning experiences. The goals of the national technology standards, just as they are for Common Core Academic Standards, apply to all students in all classrooms across the country equally. All students must have regular access to technology and the teachings that help them connect the technology to what they are learning.

Are all your students given regular access to technology to support their learning? Why or why not? This issue is an appropriate topic for department and team conversations if learning is equable and student centered and success for all students is the goal.

Lesson 3

Teacher's content expertise matters. To use technology to support learning, teachers must have a deep understanding of their content and its structure and knowledge of the essential learning and key concepts in their bailiwick.

It is understood that when teaching a new curriculum or subject, a teacher cannot be expected to know and understand all the essential concepts and key understandings that must be taught first, second, and third to build knowledge in the discipline. Over time, teachers know what must be mastered and where connections to prior knowledge and big ideas intersect. This knowledge gives teachers insights into possible scenarios where the tools and applications of technology will help students build and demonstrate their understanding.

Teacher as learner takes on critical importance as teachers become skilled at using different tools that support learning. With time and practice, a teacher knows when a video clip or movie segment will give perspective to introduce a unit on ecosystems or when a YouTube video that shows examples of propaganda being used in marketing today is timely and appropriate.

A lesson on writing thesis statements, available in the form of a cartoon, could help reteach this concept in a way that resonates and connects with students.

In each instance, the teacher must know what the key concepts, understandings, and goals are so they can apply technology to support learning. Students shouldn't just be entertained by technology. They must see the relevance to the subject matter or learning goals of using technology options.

Ask yourself where you are in integrating instruction and technology:

- What applications do you use regularly and for what purposes?
- Have you created unit plans that indicate which curriculum standards are being met and which technology standards could be embedded in lessons?
- Are there activities that could easily be modified to include digital tools or applications?

Embedded in these curricular and instructional conversations are insights into your practice and, just maybe, new goals for professional learning. Learning is social. We learn better when we can talk about what we're learning, ask questions, ask for help or support, try the new learning out and get feedback, share successes or failures, and laugh about what happened. Then figure out what worked and why.

It's not enough to drop a new tool into your teaching. Telling your students why the tool or application will support the work they are doing and modeling what is expected adds congruence to their practice and heightens the probability that the learning you are expecting will happen. A new diet or exercise program works better when you do it with a friend and hold each other accountable; the same goes for learning to use a new resource.

Lesson 4

Technology keeps evolving. Professional training is critical for teachers and staff in order for them to be current in technology use and to maximize the available technological resources. Technology needs to be used to support specific instructional purposes. Training opportunities and options must meet teachers where their needs are. Like any learning, whole school faculty in-services and workshops often aren't differentiated enough to provide the level of instruction needed. Other more informal, personalized options lend themselves to ongoing learning that builds expertise.

- Check with others on the team in the school to see which teachers are using which tools effectively and are willing to model and collaborate together.
- Investigate free resources and materials; ask the library-media or technology specialist how to evaluate the resources found and where they are best used, then do individual study.
- Collaborate with teammates and try out tools, products, and applications.
- Start a book study of a book such as *Blogs, Wikis, Podcasts, and Other Powerful Web Tools for Classrooms* by Will Richardson.

As with any learning plan, the instruction needs to fit the needs of the learner. Differentiating professional development options and opportunities moves away from a one-size-fits-all dynamic and creates those learning opportunities that actually make a difference.

Lesson 5

Valuable resources are readily available and are often free for use in classrooms to support learning. Don't let lack of funds be an obstacle. The cost to you is in the time you spend to investigate the various tools and applications your school or district subscribes to or that you've heard about. Most technology you're wondering about is defined and described online, accessed by a simple Google search, and free to classroom teachers. Not sure where to start looking for tools and applications that might work for you?

Free, educational tools and applications abound. Check these out:

- National Science Digital Library.
- Google for Educators and Google Docs or a similar tool.
- American Association of Schools Librarians' top twenty-five tech tool sites. Found at , check under Administrator to find a list of the top "25 Best Web-sites" for teaching and learning. These all meet the American Library Association's high standards, are free, and support active participation, creativity, collaboration, and learning.
- Connexions, , is a site where educators can view and share small modules. This site is housed at Rice University.
- WISE, a web-based inquiry science environment, is housed at the University of California at Berkeley and contains learning modules about real-world scientific controversies for students in grades 5–12 to read, debate, investigate, and examine.

Lesson 6

Teach and expect responsible use of technology. Safe, ethical, responsible use of technology must be part of a school or district's overall code of conduct. District policies on privileges, responsibilities, and consequences for use and misuse of technology must be clear and must be widely communicated. Post expectations for responsible use of technology in handbooks, in student use contracts that parents sign, and on posters around the school as part of the larger behavioral expectations framework. Make the language clear and understandable. There must be nothing ambiguous in the language. As Will Richardson (2009) writes, "Safety is now about responsibility, appropriateness, and common sense as well . . . it's our obligation to teach them what is acceptable and safe and what isn't" (p. 11).

If teachers expect students to understand and respect issues of privacy, copyright laws, e-mail etiquette, and the concept of public domain and know what to do if they come across something inappropriate when online, explicit training must be provided and reinforced. Talk about bullying and cyber bullying. Point out how and why using the web supports learning. If your district or school does not have a responsible use curriculum, check out the standards and ideas on the American Association of School Librarians website. Ask another district. Check with your state's department of education. Tell parents about Common Sense Media and let them review the digital citizenship curriculum they might use at home with their children to support the teaching-learning-technology connections. Here are three sites that provide simple overviews that might be helpful:

1. From Stanford University: http://fairuse.stanford.edu/;
2. From the Center for Social Media at American University: http://www.centerforsocialmedia.org/fair-use; and
3. From the North Carolina Department of Public Instruction, Wise Owl: http://www.ncwiseowl.org/zones/copyright/Student%20Guidelines.html.

Talk to students about online safety and expectations. Talk with parents, tell them what you expect, then send permission letters that state which tools and applications students will be using and why. Sample letters like the Generic Web Publication Form (Tool 5.1), and Google Apps for Education Agreement (Tool 5.2), both found in the appendix, will help you design school or district-wide permission forms.

Share information, reinforce expectations, give examples from your own use, and make learning about responsible use and safety just how you do business to build for success. Keep safety front and center as you and your students work forward.

What do these six lessons have in common? Teachers are key; systematic planning and ongoing professional support is critical; and accountability for transforming practice must be nonnegotiable. For long-term sustainability, technology must be embedded in learning across the disciplines. Along the way, operational efficiencies can be maximized using various tools and applications to free up time and money so teachers can learn to use the emerging technologies to enhance, extend, and support learning.

Whether you are the department chair, a volunteer leading a technology standing committee, or part of the school council, knowing these six lessons is only a first step. The next is to say, "So what? What now? What does this mean for us as a teaching and learning organization?" and work your way forward.

THE NEW NORMAL

Dear Jan: After teaching for five years, I was lucky enough to be a stay at home dad for the last three years. I'm back now in my fifth–sixth-grade class and so much has changed while I was gone! It has only been three years! How can this be? Isn't anything the same anymore?

The exponential multiplication of knowledge, the technological changes, the immediate access to information, the sharing of information and personal data, and the mandate that all students achieve academically at a high level as evidenced by a series of standardized tests has shifted what happens in schools. There is a new normal that is firmly embedded in this core premise—schools are about teaching and learning so that all students are successful.

Realize that premise relies on relationships and engagement between the teachers and their subjects, the teachers and their students, and the teachers and the community in which they practice. While the world moves forward at sometimes seemingly warped speed, building those critical relationships facilitates deep engagement with meaningful content, concepts, ideas, and knowledge and students and grounds the student-centered learning approach.

Indeed, teachers have had to change and adapt. Their roles and responsibilities have shifted and evolved with time and circumstance. Traditional teachers' methods and approaches must change if teachers are to meet the challenges necessary for implementing and maintaining appropriate academic rigor for each and every student in light of the various complex factors (economics, diversity, class size to name a few) impacting education today.

So while you may find what you do as a teacher has changed, the goal has not. Your goal is to help all students be successful learners. This should have been true three years ago, but check in with your teammates or team leader and get a sense of what's affecting the currents in your educational environment and how you can swiftly adapt.

Consider the following: Traditionally, the role of teachers has been as a dispenser of information and person in control of what students are learning (content). In that scenario, students were often the passive receiver and, as such, were either successful or unsuccessful. Period.

No longer are the textbook and the teacher the sole sources for information, nor is the classroom the only place where content learning occurs. Learning has become more fluid and complex. The roles and responsibilities of both the teacher and the student have changed as a result.

Here's where you might approach whatever team you are on and ask about the evolving teaching-learning paradigm. This will help illuminate the shift in roles and responsibilities. The Teacher Roles and Reflections Chart, Tool 5.3 in the appendix, is one you and the team might read, discuss, analyze, and consider as a model as you think about the broader roles teachers assume so that all students become successful learners.

Through discussion, you'll be able to add more specificity to the descriptors and discover if only the role labels have changed; many of these you may be familiar with and do automatically.

As teachers become the resource (whose expertise targets the learning outcomes and pinpoints the concepts, skills, and knowledge that direct any given unit of study), students become participants in how learning is shaped. Students take on more responsibility for learning, for meeting targets, and for how that learning will be accomplished. Students call this "more freedom," teachers call it "engaged ownership."

The labels and descriptors in Tool 5.3, found in the appendix, reflect today's new normal as a result of the shift in understanding teaching and learning to meet the needs of today's students and the world they will inherit. Knowing and understanding this critical shift is where students and teachers come together to design active, interesting, and engaging learning.

When students assume more accountability for their learning, their roles shift and change as well. The Student Roles chart, Tool 5.4 in the appendix, describes those shifts. The goal remains the same: for all students to be successful academically.

As teachers or a team of teachers, you might consider sharing the student chart with students so they know what is expected of them. Some of the roles are self-explanatory; others need more definition or a set of examples that flesh out the intent. The goal is to give students a clear vision of what independent, engaged, and effective learners look like. That's what your team of teachers is working toward, effectively meeting the learning needs of students today!

At the core of this new normal is a school where teaching and learning and academic success are linked and where skilled teachers have relationships with their students, their content, and with each other as a team of professionals that allows them to develop partnerships that advance student learning. The labels may have changed but the idea of schools as communities of learning is stronger than ever!

AGENTS OF CHANGE

Dear Jan: How can we teacher leaders empower our various teams to be agents of meaningful and mindful change?

The leader's challenge is to mobilize everyone in their organization, especially those who are the front line, to come together for a shared purpose. This should be based on trust and the belief that by working together we strengthen and improve our professional practices. We have the same goal, for our students to learn at a consistently high level.

Teachers are the front line; what happens with teaching and learning resides squarely on their shoulders. They must know that what they do matters.

As you know, the classrooms you and your colleagues walk into every day are filled with a rich tapestry of diversity, students who are gifted, language challenged, disenfranchised, interested, poor, and for some, displaced. For all to succeed to thrive and not just put in seat time, teacher leaders and their teams are pivotal. In that educational onion, you are closest to the center, your students.

As Doug Reeves writes in *Leading Change in Your School* (2009), "Few leverage points have the greatest influence on student achievement: teaching, professional learning, collaboration and time (including meetings)" (p. 57).

As the leader of a team of teachers, it's important to acknowledge that, indeed, what once worked is shifting, sometimes a full 360 degrees. Today, the very essence of teaching and learning must shift to meet the learning needs of students whose tomorrow is no longer predictable.

So what empowers teachers to work hard and make sure that what they are doing is meaningful and fulfilling? Look again at the components of leadership: *Effective teacher leaders create the conditions for others' success by building relationships to support teaching and learning.*

When teachers know that the work they are doing in their team will impact what goes on with their students in their classrooms, engagement happens.

Motivation rises when teachers have a say in what will be studied and are able to influence decisions and timelines and have a say in what will be changed, studied, or moved, and in the processes involved.

When leaders throughout the organization believe learning is *the* core activity, they position teams to practice inquiry together, to consider ideas and alternatives, to try things out, to analyze results, and to be creative in tackling the complexities of teaching and learning. This can be energizing work.

What can a teacher leader do? Acknowledge that what you and the team are doing is important work. Take time to talk with one another, share stories of success and trials, laugh, and find the time to play together. Make the work of the team count and let everyone know they make a difference. Being appreciated for showing up and working diligently should count for something.

Being told that your contributions make us all stronger/better/smarter is energizing. Being asked, "What would you do?" "How would you approach this?" "Can you help me figure this out?" all say you matter here. Those genuine acknowledgments go a long way in building relationships that will support the work being done.

Where else might a team start? Pull three tools: Framing Student Centered Learning, Tool 1.1; Taking Promising Practices to Scale, Tool 2.2;

and Establishing New Learning Environments, Tool 4.3; and use these tools to compare and illuminate practices that bring students into the learning equation as active partners and to act as a catalyst for team conversation. Listen to the talents and skills others bring to the team's collective table and be interested in how each can contribute to the team's repertoire.

Ask your teammates:

- What do we have in place that reflects the elements of these frameworks?
- What do we have to stop doing or change to implement practices to engage all students?
- What will a thorough assessment of current practice entail, and where do we need help in understanding and moving forward on any element?
- Are we fully committed to doing this together, using our time in this way? If not, what must occur so that we make this commitment?

As the teacher leader, practice learning in action by modeling inquiry using whatever approach you choose. Sometimes it's about asking the questions to which there are no readily available answers. Empowerment is about ensuring that all the teachers on the team have a voice to ask what we have tried, how it worked, and what I/we could do differently to make learning meaningful so all students are learning. Voice, choice, and relationships are key elements when creating the conditions for others' success.

Teacher leaders whose leadership style encourages all members to actively examine practice know the power in celebrations. Celebrations about real, meaningful work, contributions, or accomplishments say loud and clear that our work matters. Inspiring.

Empowerment comes from believing the whole is stronger than the parts, that isolation and disenfranchised employees weaken our work as a collection of talents. Teams that have a shared responsibility to purpose and each other and have the ability to set goals that are important to their work with their students are productive and engaged.

Building a vibrant learning community extends to the adults as well as students in today's school; that's critical because the future of our students relies on the collection of adults who understand the complexities of change and the challenges inherent in teaching and learning. They know students' success is in their hands.

Leadership that engages teachers in meaningful, sustainable work to strength their collective practice is that essential. That leadership, where what teachers do matters, is the catalyst for meaningful motivation and change. It is about possibilities. Teacher leaders are the directors.

CONVERSATION STARTERS

1. Reread the paragraph above that begins with "Building a vibrant learning community." How did you react to that paragraph when you read it? Did it challenge and inspire you? How will you use that to work with your team to meet the goals and needs inherent in your school and classrooms? Define and discuss.
2. Did any of the six technology lessons surprise you? How are you and the team keeping up with digital and electronic changes? At what point are you involving students and parents in your use of these lessons to support teaching and learning? How are you doing this?
3. What surprised you about the teacher- and student-roles charts, Tools 5.3 and 5.4? What was not listed that should be? How different is this set of roles from what you do currently? Have you considered using the Student Roles chart (Tool 5.4) with students? If so, how did that go and was it useful?
4. A number of leadership themes were woven throughout the book. Identify several that support your current work and discuss their implications for you as a teacher and for your team of teachers. What area will you devote more time and research to? What do you hope to find? What reoccurring theme will most impact your practice and how will you go about keeping that in your sights as the year progresses?

ADDITIONAL INFORMATION ON SHIFTS AND CHANGE

- Wenger, McDermott and Snyder's 2002 book *Cultivating Communities of Practice: A Guide to Managing Knowledge* is a great resource when investigating the *whats, hows* and *whys* of knowledge-oriented structures, for that is truly what teams are about.
- Two books are worthy of a leadership book study; both will impact what teacher leaders and others do with their schools and teams. Michael Fullan's *Leading in a Culture of Change* and Doug Reeves's *Leading Change in Your School* are illuminating.
- The International Society for Technology Education is a nonprofit professional organization dedicated to providing leadership and service to improve teaching and learning by advancing the effective use of technology in K–12 education and teacher education. ISTE provides information on networking opportunities, as guidance to incorporating computers, the Internet, and other new technologies into schools. www.iste.org.

Appendix

LIST OF TOOLS

Tool 1.1   Framework for Student Centered Learning
Tool 2.1   Professional Learning Communities Survey
Tool 2.2   Taking Promising High School Practices to Scale
Tool 2.3   Framing Content, Process, and Product
Tool 2.4   Teacher Leader's Feedback Survey
Tool 3.1   Our Core Values Protocol
Tool 3.2   Four P's for Organized Learning
Tool 4.1   Case Study Protocol
Tool 4.2   Marzano's Taxonomy Chart
Tool 4.3   Establishing New Learning Environments Chart
Tool 4.4   Self-Reflection Exercise
Tool 5.1   Generic Web Publications Form
Tool 5.2   Sample Google Apps for Education Agreement
Tool 5.3   Teacher Roles and Reflections Chart
Tool 5.4   Student Roles

TOOL 1.1: FRAMEWORK FOR STUDENT CENTERED LEARNING

SEVEN COMPONENTS FOR STUDENT CENTERED LEARNING

1: Culture:
Intentionally build a vibrant learning community.
2: Structure:
Create structures and systems that support learning.
3: Rigor:
Implement a rigorous, academic curriculum.
4: Engagement:
Select and connect best practices to engage students and meet individual needs.
5: Technology:
Leverage technology to enhance, extend, and expand learning opportunities and options.
6: Essential Skills:
Embed essential skills across disciplines.
7: Assessment:
Use multiple formal and informal assessments regularly to check for understanding.

Appendix

TOOL 2.1: PROFESSIONAL LEARNING COMMUNITIES SURVEY

National School Reform Faculty
Harmony Education Center www.nsrfharmony.org

Professional Learning Communities Survey

Based on the article: Building Professional Community in Schools by Sharon Kruse, Karen Seashore Louis and Anthony Bryk.

This survey will help you think about and assess the extent to which each of the major factors associated with professional learning community—critical elements, human resources, and structural conditions is currently present at your school.

1.0 CRITICAL ELEMENTS

1.1 Reflective Dialogue
   a. Faculty/staff members talk with each other about their situations and the specific challenges they face.

Not at All	Somewhat	50%	To a large Degree	To a Great Extent
1	2	3	4	5

1.2 De-Privatization of Practice
   b. Teachers share, observe, & discuss each others' teaching methods & philosophies.

Not at All	Somewhat	50%	To a large Degree	To a Great Extent
1	2	3	4	5

1.3 Collective Focus on Student Learning
   c. Teachers assume that all students can learn at reasonably high levels & that teachers can help them.

Not at All	Somewhat	50%	To a large Degree	To a Great Extent
1	2	3	4	5

1.4 Collaboration
   d. Teachers not only work together to develop shared understandings of students, curriculum & instructional policy, but also produce materials & activities that improve instruction, curriculum, & assessment.

Not at All	Somewhat	50%	To a large Degree	To a Great Extent
1	2	3	4	5

1.5 Shared Norms and Values
   e. Through words & actions teachers affirm their common values concerning critical educational issues and in support of their collective focus on student learning.

Not at All	Somewhat	50%	To a large Degree	To a Great Extent
1	2	3	4	5

Protocols are most powerful and effective when used within an ongoing professional learning community such as a Critical Friends Group® and facilitated by a skilled coach. To learn more about professional learning communities and seminars for new or experienced coaches, please visit the National School Reform Faculty website at www.nsrfharmony.org.

2.0 HUMAN RESOURCES

2.1 Openness to Improvement
a. Teachers take risks in trying new techniques and ideas and make efforts to learn more about their profession.

Not at All	Somewhat	50%	To a large Degree	To a Great Extent
1	2	3	4	5

2.2 Trust and Respect
b. Teachers feel honored for their expertise within the school as well as within the district, the parent community and other significant groups.

Not at All	Somewhat	50%	To a large Degree	To a Great Extent
1	2	3	4	5

2.3 Cognitive and Skill Base
c. Within the school there are formal methods for sharing expertise among faculty members so that marginal and ineffective teachers can improve.

Not at All	Somewhat	50%	To a large Degree	To a Great Extent
1	2	3	4	5

2.4 Supportive Leadership
d. The school leadership keeps the school focused on shared purpose, continuous improvement, and collaboration.

Not at All	Somewhat	50%	To a large Degree	To a Great Extent
1	2	3	4	5

2.5 Socialization
e. The staff imparts a sense that new teachers are an important and productive part of a meaningful school community.

Not at All	Somewhat	50%	To a large Degree	To a Great Extent
1	2	3	4	5

3.0 STRUCTURAL CONDITIONS

3.1 Time to Meet and Talk
a. There is a formal process that provides substantial & regularly scheduled blocks of time for educators to conduct on-going self-examination & self-renewal.

Not at All	Somewhat	50%	To a large Degree	To a Great Extent
1	2	3	4	5

3.2 Physical Proximity
b. Teachers have common spaces, rooms, or areas for discussion of educational practices.

Not at All	Somewhat	50%	To a large Degree	To a Great Extent
1	2	3	4	5

Protocols are most powerful and effective when used within an ongoing professional learning community such as a Critical Friends Group® and facilitated by a skilled coach. To learn more about professional learning communities and seminars for new or experienced coaches, please visit the National School Reform Faculty website at www.nsrfharmony.org.

Appendix

3.3 Interdependent Teaching Roles
c. There are recurring formal situations in which teachers work together (team teaching, integrated lessons etc.)

Not at All	Somewhat	50%	To a large Degree	To a Great Extent
1	2	3	4	5

3.4 Communication Structures
d. There are structures & opportunities for an <u>exchange</u> of ideas, both within and across such organizational units as teams, grade levels, & subject departments.

Not at All	Somewhat	50%	To a large Degree	To a Great Extent
1	2	3	4	5

3.5 Teacher Empowerment & School Autonomy
e. Teachers have autonomy to make decisions regarding their work guide by the norms and beliefs of the professional community.

Not at All	Somewhat	50%	To a large Degree	To a Great Extent
1	2	3	4	5

Protocols are most powerful and effective when used within an ongoing professional learning community such as a Critical Friends Group® and facilitated by a skilled coach. To learn more about professional learning communities and seminars for new or experienced coaches, please visit the National School Reform Faculty website at www.nsrfharmony.org.

From National School Reform Faculty/NSRF

TOOL 2.2: TAKING PROMISING HIGH SCHOOL PRACTICES TO SCALE

COMPARISON OF TRADITIONAL AND PROFICIENCY-BASED SECONDARY EDUCATION

	Traditional	Proficiency-Based
View of Learners	Some will excel, some will do average work, a portion will fail.	All of them can achieve at high standards; failure is not an option.
Learning Program	Time based; learning is a variable. It's effective for a portion of students	Learning based; time is a variable. It's effective for all students.
Grades	Based on various, and sometimes subjective, points rather than proficiencies; may reflect quantity over quality (such as extra credit work); may be used in part to punish, reward, or control student behavior; subject to inflation. Grades are sometimes locked in before a course ends.	Indicate only what student has learned (knows and can do) by demonstration of proficiency; quality of work is based on agreements about evidence of proficiency. End-of-course grades reflect student proficiency *at* end of course.
Assessment	Relies heavily on summative assessment, including standardized testing.	Includes summative assessment, but heavily favors formative assessment as a feedback mechanism to continuously measure and guide student learning, and to drive and improve instruction.
Nature and Structure of Schools	Often adult centered in practice. Self-contained education factories in a management hierarchy modeled on 20th Century industry.	Student centered in practice. Home base for flexible learning experiences where students can assume more initiative, work in teams, and learn in community settings, online venues, and other education institutions as well as in their school of record.
Curriculum	Disciplines are independent of one another and content is independent of standards for postsecondary success.	Based on recognized standards. Rigor and relevance are driving criteria. Disciplines are often integrated. Content is keyed to what students need for postsecondary studies and job success.
Student Credentialing	Students accumulate graded units of instruction to graduate through "seat time," regardless of skill levels acquired or grades assigned, and a standard diploma is regarded as the end point of the high school experience. For students capable of doing more and advancing while still in high school, the senior year is often spent coasting to the finish line.	Students are assessed to assure that they have acquired high standards of knowledge and skills defined by minimum state diploma requirements matched to state standards. Students with an interest in advanced certification and credits (AP, IB, college credits) are supported in going beyond minimum diploma requirements.
Teachers	They dispense knowledge about subject matter; lead class discussion, make assignments, motivate students, assign grades.	They do many of the traditional things but also are content experts, mentors, resources, partners in school management, partners with community resource providers, skilled assessment practitioners, members of teaching teams, and members of professional learning communities.
Students	They receive or absorb information passively, recite when asked, achieve on tests. Often don't know at the beginning of a course what constitutes successful learning.	They envision and help plan their education path, partner in their own progress, learn by observation and application as well as by reading and taking class notes, and they develop both individual and group skills. From the very beginning of a course, they know precisely what proficiencies demonstrate desired attainment of knowledge and skills, and they work to achieve those proficiencies.
Student Performance Data	Infrequently collected and analyzed, if at all.	Frequently collected and analyzed (currently and longitudinally) by teachers, professional learning communities, and curriculum and instruction administrators for program improvement.

From 2009 Oregon Business Council Education White Paper

TOOL 2.3: FRAMING CONTENT, PROCESS, AND PRODUCT

Teachers have many decisions to make over the course of any teaching day. Primary are the *what, how, when* decisions they make for curriculum, instruction, and assessment to accommodate learning. Three critical decision points are:

- Content—what kind and how much content a student studies;
- Process—way in which the student learns; and
- Product—nature of how the student demonstrates learning.

Before determining how a student will proceed with learning, the student's learning needs must be established. Once the student's learning needs have been properly identified, the discussion centers around exploring the Content, Process, and Product option for learning the content. Ideas like these might emerge:

- How about if you just work with this piece of content? When you finish with this, then we can choose something else. [Content]
- Because you passed the pretest at 92 percent, let's pinpoint the area that'll bring you to 100 percent. Then, what do you think about us setting up an independent study project for you? [Process]
- I can extend the time you have to complete your work but before I do, we need to make sure you have a plan in place for completing high quality work by the deadline we both agree fits your needs. [Process]
- I have developed five different ways to learn this content. Look these over and see which one appeals to you. It is also possible to combine elements of each and create a new option. Let me know what you decide. [Content and Process]
- Choose one of these three vehicles to showcase what you learned: demonstration, a storyboard, or a web-designed interactive game, and let's meet to fine tune the details. [Product]
- After you show 80 percent mastery of the unit, choose one concept and develop that into a visual display of your choosing. That display must encompass the critical elements of the concept you chose. [Product]

TOOL 2.4: TEACHER LEADER'S FEEDBACK SURVEY

Below I have listed areas of responsibility I have in my role as teacher leader. I am interested in gathering your feedback to help me reflect on and strengthen my leadership. Please give specific examples where you believe I excel and also identify areas needing more attention or training. This feedback will help me set goals so that our work together is productive.

Thank you in advance for your thoughtful responses. Feel free to sign your name or drop this off in my mailbox anonymously.

Responsibility #1: [*example: Communication*]
Feedback: [*I value the quick turnaround of team minutes and the notes about who has what follow up responsibility. I also like that when there is a question or concern I should know about, you come to me directly. Helps me know you care and are there for support. I wish we had more time to really talk about instruction; sometimes we just talk an issue to death.*]

Responsibility #2:
Feedback:

Responsibility #3:
Feedback:

Responsibility #4:
Feedback:

Responsibility #5:
Feedback:

Please return to me by _____. Thanks.

TOOL 3.1: OUR CORE VALUES PROTOCOL

Purpose: to allow a team or school to identify core values/beliefs each member holds and to develop a set of community values that are visible and present and provide clarity and direction to our work.
Materials: chart paper, pencils/pens and space in which to work, 1½ hours, snacks/water.
Procedure: Read and follow the steps 1–7 below.

Step 1 (5 minutes)

Explain that values are behaviors that underscore what we believe and how we make decisions.

In this activity, make believe we are setting up our ideal team/school. We want to help all our students be successful as a result of our faculty behaviors, skills, and desires. Therefore, having a set of identified core values to help us make decisions will be imperative to our mission. It's important to our work that we narrow down and agree on 6–8 values that will guide our work long term.

Step 2 (5–10 minutes)

All participants brainstorm behaviors, qualities, and characteristics telling what you would want members of your new school/team to have. You will probably list about 50 terms like: integrity, leadership, ability to learn, compassion, initiative, competency, and the like.

Step 3 (15 minutes)

Divide the participants into groups of 4. Each group is to come to consensus around 6–8 of the qualities listed as core values.

Step 4 (5–15 minutes)

Groups share their 6–8 values and a facilitator puts a check mark as a tally as groups report back to the larger group. The chart reflects the total from the set of participants. The top 6–8 values are circled. Highlight the values that emerged. Ask: what does this tell you about our group that you might not have known before? Any surprises? What would it take for us to use these as we work together and with our learning community?

Step 5 (10–20 minutes)

Each individual now considers the top 6–8 values and answers the following three statements for each value. After every member has answered all three questions for the set of values, groups of 4 discuss each in turn. All participants have a chance to share their answers with their group.
For each value, answer the following:
1. Describe what _____(value) means to you.
2. Describe the behaviors that illustrate this value.
3. If we adopt this value, what will be the results that follow?

(If time is running short for the exercise, decide whether it makes sense to continue or end the session and continue at the next opportunity. If ending, ask each participant to consider what they wrote and bring it to the next meeting and in the following days be mindful of their work and the core values they have described. They will have a chance to relook at their top 6–8 descriptions for refinement at the next meeting.)

If continuing: Step 6 (15–30 minutes)

Call on different members of different groups (randomly) to share what was written about the various values. Ask if others want to expand the descriptions. Allow additions if they stay on topic and add to the understanding of the core belief/value.

After reviewing the descriptors for all 6–8 core values, tell the participants you will ask them to be mindful of these values as you move forward, that they will be written up with descriptions and that you all will consider these values again as a faculty over the next number of months. They are to guide your work and your decisions. When teams or the faculty meet, intentionally use them to guide/reflect your work.

Core values should be revisited from time to time to assure the group that these core values are indeed what we believe and use to guide our decisions. If one or another of the values doesn't work over time, bring all participants together and discuss why this one might need to be changed, broadened, or abandoned.

Step 7 (5 minutes)

Each participant answers the following on a slip of paper to turn in as he or she exits the meeting:

What did you think of this activity? How will the results be useful in guiding your work as a member of a team and our faculty? What next steps would help you integrate these core values into your work within our larger learning community?

Finally, do share the answers with all participants via a bulleted document, no names. When you have the final agreed-upon set of values, list them at the top of faculty communiqués so that they are dynamic and carry weight.

TOOL 3.2: FOUR P'S FOR ORGANIZED LEARNING

The Four Ps are:

- Establish a culture where relationships and high expectations exist between teachers and students. [*Personal*]
- Create an operational structure consistent for both teachers and students where both are expected to assume responsibility for the environment. [*Predictable*]
- Maintain a learning environment that is creative, inviting, safe, well organized, and student centered. [*Productive*]
- Plan intentionally so consistency, processes, and structures support meaningful cognitive engagement. [*Purposeful*]

Learning Communities

- Productive
- Personal
- Predictable

- Purposeful

TOOL 4.1: CASE STUDY PROTOCOL

Purpose: to probe an issue, question, or dilemma that you have run up against and for which you need perspective or guidance. Team members are invited to bring burning questions to the group as case studies on a regularly scheduled basis.
Time: 30–45 minutes.
Materials: one copy of the case study and any supporting documents for each team member.
Procedure: The facilitator convenes the group by reviewing the agreements for case study work. These are generally set up prior to anyone bringing an actual case study to the group. [listen actively, ask clarifying or probing questions, share the floor, be respectful, no interruptions] If your team is new to case studies work, use a question or dilemma that is generative to allow the team to work through a couple of sample scenarios to build understanding and comfort. Then provide regular team time to build support for the group's members.

Sample Case Study

How do you, as team leader, move the conversation from more managerial work to teaching and learning or exploring a new approach as a team?

1. A written case study, no longer than one page, is presented to the team. The case study sets the context and describe the circumstances so others understand the dilemma. The case study ends with a question posed for the group to consider. The question should probe others' thinking and not be answered by a yes or no. "My students like big projects and I'm letting them help decide what those should be, but they don't seem to do so well on end of unit writing exams. How do I better connect their various projects with the targets I have in mind and still let them feel they had a choice in all this? Their writing scores are only average at best."

    You might share your instructions for the writing exam and a couple of pieces of student work.
2. Members each ask one clarifying or probing question as you go around the circle but no one is to offer advice or a fix. Use *Tell me more about . . . Why do you think . . . How would understanding the writing criteria have influenced . . . What evidence are you basing your conclusion on? How was this presented?*
3. The presenter reflects back what he or she heard and either thanks the group or, if comfortable, shares how he or she is now looking at

the issue or question. "I'm thinking that if I changed how I structured the lesson and shared the three learning goals up front, my students might have designed their projects in a way they could hit the target I was looking for."

It is important the presenter feels safe to share his or her case as it is meaningful to that person. The group must avoid telling the presenter what to do to fix the case or offer *if I were you I'd . . .* advice.

4. At some later time, the team leader checks in with the presenter to see if the process was helpful and whether he or she wants another round with the group.

TOOL 4.2: MARZANO'S TAXONOMY: QUESTIONING FACT SHEET

From Charlotte-Mecklenburg School District

Level of Thinking Skill	Processes Involved	Verbs Involved	Question Stems to Use
Knowing	Focusing on needed information Defining the problem Setting goals for solving problems Obtaining information through the senses Formulating questions for inquiry Storing information in long-term memory Recalling information from long-term memory	Categorize Group Classify Compare Contrast	Who did __? When was __? What is ___? Indentify the __ in the __. Describe Which _ best defines__? Which _ is characteristic of _? Which _ is an example of _?
Organizing	Comparison—noting similarities and differences Classifying—grouping and labeling entities Ordering—sequencing entities by a criterion Representing—changing the form but not the substance of information	Categorize Group Classify Compare Contrast	Categorize _ according to __. Classify __ according to __. How is __ alike or different from __? What is most (or least) important about __? In your own words, tell __.
Applying	Using information for practical purposes Demonstrating prior knowledge within a new situation Bringing together	Apply Make Show Record Construct Demonstrate	Give some instance which __? How is __ related to __? How is __ an example of __? How would you use this information?

Appendix

	appropriate information for problems Using generalizations to solve problems	Illustrate	What do you need to solve this problem? What are possible solutions to __?
Analyzing	Clarifying information by studying parts and relationships Identifying attributes and components Determining the characteristics of an entity Identifying relationships and patterns Identify the main idea or central element Establishing the hierarchy of key ideas Identifying errors and logical fallacies	Outline Diagram Differentiate Analyze	What are the attributes of __? What evidence can you list for __? What are the components, parts or features of __? What patterns or relationships do you see in __? Outline, web, or diagram __. What are the main ideas __? What can be concluded about __?
Generating	Producing new information, meaning, or ideas Inferring—going beyond available information Predicting—anticipating next events or outcomes Elaborating—explaining by adding additional details, examples, or other relevant information	Conclude Predict Infer Explain Elaborate	How many ways can you think of to __? What would happen if __? Predict what would be true if __. How can you explain __? Elaborate about __. What would you predict/infer from __? What solutions would you suggest for __? If you were __, how would you have __?
Integrating	Connecting and combining information Summarizing—restructuring information efficiently Restructuring—changing existing knowledge structures to incorporate new information	Combine Summarize Design Imagine Generalize	Devise a plan to __. Summarize __. How many ways can you think of to __? Conclude what the result would be if __. What generalizations can you make? If you could pull this all together in 3–4 sentences, what would you say?
Evaluating	Assessing the reasonableness and quality of ideas Establishing criteria for judging	Judge Evaluate Rate Verify Assess	What do you think about __? Why? Which __ is most significant and why? What are your sources? How

Verifying the accuracy of claims	Define criteria	do you know they are credible? Do you detect any biases? Judge what would be the best way to __. What criteria did you use? What is your point of view about this? Are there other points of view about this? How effective was __?

TOOL 4.3: ESTABLISHING NEW LEARNING ENVIRONMENTS/INCORPORATING NEW STRATEGIES

Traditional Learning Environments	New Learning Environments
Teacher-center instruction	Student-centered instruction
Single-sense stimulation	Multisensory stimulation
Single media	Multimedia
Isolated work	Collaborative work
Information delivery	Information exchange
Passive learning	Active/exploratory/inquiry-based learning
Factual, knowledge-based learning	Critical thinking and informed decision making
Reactive response	Proactive/planned action
Isolated, artificial context	Authentic, real-world context

TOOL 4.4: SELF-REFLECTION EXERCISE

Self-reflection is critical to improving professional practice. This exercise is designed to help you understand the impact of your decisions and help you determine next steps. Find a quiet place where you can think carefully about the questions being asked and record your answers so you can refer back to them as needed. You might consider sharing your thoughts with a colleague you trust.

1. Write a description of the experience or activity.
2. Identify the key issues that are on your mind.
3. Answer the following questions based on the decisions you made at that time.
    - What 3 words best describe my thinking when I started this reflection?
    - How did it go?

- How did I feel during the experience or process?
- What factors influenced my decisions and actions?
- Were there other factors I should have considered?
- If so, what were they?
- How might that have changed the outcome?
- How do I feel now?
- What new information will I take from this reflection and how will this inform my decisions and action next time?

4. If I do this another time, what support or resources do I need and where can I find them?

TOOL 5.1: GENERIC WEB PUBLICATIONS FORM

Your School District Letterhead
Your School

Parent Permission Form for Web Publication of Student Work

Name of Student
Name of Parent
School Year for Which Permission is Given
Class for Which Permission is Given
We understand that our daughter/son is completing projects in class that may be published on the web (blogs, video sharing sites such as YouTube or other venues where students may share work). No home address or telephone number will appear with such work. Students may choose at times to put first and/or last names on the work they post.
I grant permission for my student to post his/her work as described above.
Yes No
I also grant permission for my daughter's or son's first and last name to be published along with his/her work, if he or she chooses.
Yes No
Parent Signature Date
Parent Name (Printed)
I, the student, also give my permission for my work to be published.
Student Signature Date
Student Name (Printed)
Note: Sample letter written by Garnetta Wilker, retired librarian, Oregon Trail School District, Sandy, Oregon.

TOOL 5.2: SAMPLE GOOGLE APPS FOR EDUCATION AGREEMENT

School letterhead/date.

This year, _____ High School will be using Google Apps for Education in the classroom. Google Apps for Education is a suite of free, web-based programs that include email, document creation, shared calendars, and collaboration tools.

Please review the Google Apps information available at registration or on our district website; complete and return this permission page to school. If you have any questions, please don't hesitate to call the school at #

_____

Student name: _____
Parent/Guardian: _____

_____ I give permission for my child to use Google Apps for Education. By doing so, I agree to enforce acceptable use when my child is off District Property.

_____ I give permission for my child and the school to publish student work and photographs online, with the understanding that student last names and confidential personal information will be published.

Parent Signature Date

Note: Sample letter written by Garnetta Wilker, retired librarian, Oregon Trail School District, Sandy, Oregon.

TOOL 5.3: TEACHER ROLES AND REFLECTIONS CHART

Teacher as:	Descriptor:
Content expert	Deep understanding of critical content in my discipline, vertically and horizontally; able to prompt student thinking/inquiry
Collaborator	Seeks input, shares knowledge and expertise, listens actively, builds relationships, resolves conflicts, respectful
Coach/advocate and mentor	Provides support and guidance to students and shares expertise with teachers and team
Time manager	Understands time as a tool for learning, flexes time as needed, and teaches students to use and track time to support learning
Resource manager	Uses resources, time and people to support student learning, reaches across community
Team & faculty member	Active participant across content, freely shares knowledge and skills, supports mission and vision of student-centered model

Designer and problem solver	Creates choices, uses and models multiple strategies for identifying issues and crafting solutions
Assessor, analyzer, user of data	Knows how to use data, what data to use to improve teaching and help inform student learning
Decision maker	Selects content, matches teaching strategies, level of challenge with tools, assessments to student learning needs; has a voice in decisions about teaching/learning
Communicator	Uses multiple avenues to communicate across audiences, does so in timely and coherent and invitational fashion
Leader	Active member of the learning community, facilitates learning, shares in advancing the goals and mission of team/school
Community builder	Creates warm, engaging, safe place for learning, has systems and procedures in place that are known and followed, invites others to partner for learning
Technology facilitator	Keeps abreast with tools, matches uses to appropriate content to support learning, ongoing assessment and communication
Learner and reflective practitioner	Considers own professional growth critical for student learning and academic success, takes measured risks in teaching and learning to expand own knowledge base

TOOL 5.4: STUDENT ROLES

Student as:	Descriptor:
Leader	Using skills, talents, and expertise to help others learn
Scholar	Matching content, skills to interests and appropriate levels of thinking
Peer coach	Being supportive of peers, using knowledge and expertise to help others learn, providing positive feedback to others
Collaborator	Working with peers, content, experts, teachers, and others to impact learning
Time manager	Planning, tracking, managing work time so tasks are completed within a designated time frame
Advocate	Bringing questions, concerns, issues, and ideas forward so learning problems and stumbling blocks are resolved
Data detective	Uses feedback, analyzes formative and summative data to make adjustments in learning plans and targets
Designer	Creates a learning plan for studying content based on appropriate targets and goals
Problem solver	Identifies learning roadblocks, seeks answers to questions, frames issues, and identifies possible solutions

Communicator	Exchanges ideas, written or spoken, with others in person and across a variety of media with decorum, accepts diverse points of view, advocates for self and others, is coherent, uses words accurately, and understands nuances when using electronics
Conceptual learner	Moves learning from concrete to more abstract, takes big ideas, finds connections and patterns and strives to think and work at levels that build deeper understanding
Thinker	Uses facts to create new knowledge, identifies opinions and bias; able to analyze problems and issues and can arrive at viable alternatives and solutions
Self-Reflective	Identifies strengths and limitations, makes adjustments, aware of own processes that support learning; can use metacognitive strategies and uses formal and informal learning data

References

Ainsworth, L. (2003). *Power standards: Identifying the standards that matter the most.* Englewood, CO: Advanced Learning Press.
Arbuckle, M., Dobea, C., Harding, G., Horsley-Locks, S., Murray, L. & Williams, M. (1987). *Continuing to learn: A guidebook for teacher development.* Andover, MA, Oxford, OH: The Regional Laboratory for Educational Improvement and National Staff Development Council.
Armstrong, T. (1994). *Multiple intelligences in the classroom.* Alexandria, VA: ASCD.
Boykin, A. W. & Noguera, P. (2011). *Creating the opportunity to learn: Moving from research and practice to close the achievement gap.* Alexandria, VA.: ASCD.
Brooks, J. & Brooks, M. (1993). *In search of understanding: The case for constructivist classrooms.* Alexandria, VA: ASCD.
Burgess, J. & Bates, D. (2009). *Other duties as assigned: Tips, tools, and techniques for expert teacher leadership.* Alexandria, VA: ASCD.
Cabrera, D. & Colosi, C. (2009). *Thinking at every desk.* Ithaca, NY: Research Institute for Thinking in Education.
Caine, R. N. & Caine, G. (1997). *Education on the edge of possibility.* Alexandria, VA: ASCD.
Carr, J. & Harris, D. (2001). *Succeeding with standards: Linking curriculum, assessment and action planning.* Alexandria, VA: ASCD.
Center for Performance Assessment. (2004). *Making standards work.* Englewood, CO: Center for Performance Assessment.
Chen, M. & Rybak, C. (2004). *Group leadership skills: Interpersonal process in group counseling and therapy.* Belmont: CA: Brooks/Cole, a division of Thompson Learning.
Christenbury, L. (2010, December/2011, January). The flexible teacher. *Educational Leadership,* 68(4), 48–50.
Conley, D. (2011, March). What students need to learn. *Educational Leadership,* 68(6), 16–20.
Cookson, Peter Jr. (2009, September). What would Socrates say? *Educational Leadership,* 67(1), 8–14.
Costa, A. (2008, February). The thought-filled curriculum. *Educational Leadership,* 65(5), 20–24.
Costa, A. & Kallick, B. (Eds). (2009). *Habits of mind across the curriculum: Practical and creative strategies for teachers.* Alexandria, VA: ASCD.
Costa, A. & Kallick, B. (2009). It takes some getting used to: Rethinking curriculum for the 21st century. In H. Jacobs (Ed.), *Curriculum 21: Essential education for a changing world.* Alexandria, VA: ASCD.
Covey, S. (2009, October). A school for leadership. *Educational Leadership,* 67(2), 61–66.
Covey, S. M. & Merrill, R. (2006). *The speed of trust: The one thing that changes everything.* New York: Free Press.
Creswell, J. (1997). *Creating worlds: Constructing meaning.* Portsmouth, NH: Heinemann.
Cummings, C. (1980). *Teaching makes a difference.* Snohomish, WA: Snohomish Publishing Company.
Cummings, C., Nelson, C., & Shaw, D. (1985). *Peering in on peers: Coaching teachers.* Edmonds, WA: Teaching.
Curry, B. & Temple, T. (1992). *Using curriculum frameworks for systematic reform.* Alexandria, VA: ASCD.

References

Cushman, Kathleen. (2010, February). The striver of it: Meeting students where they are. *Educational Leadership*, 67(5), 50–55.

Cutsall, S. (2009, September). Clicking across cultures. *Educational Leadership*, 67(1), 40–44.

Danielson, C., (1996/2007). *Enhancing professional practice: A framework for teaching.* Alexandria, VA: ASCD.

Danielson, C. & McGreal, T. (2000). *Teacher evaluation: To enhance professional practice.* Alexandria, VA: ASCD.

Darling-Hammond, L. (1998, February). Teacher learning that supports student learning. *Educational Leadership*, 55(5), 6–11.

Donaldson, G. A. (2006). *Cultivating leadership in schools: Connecting people, purpose, & practice*, 2nd edition. New York: Teachers College Press.

DuFour, R. (2004, May). What is a professional learning community? *Educational Leadership*, 61(8), 6–11.

Dweck, C. (2010, September). Even geniuses work hard. *Educational Leadership*, 68(1), 16–20.

Dyak, B. A. (2010, August). Web 2.0 and you! *Middle Ground*, 38.

The effective educator. (2010, December/2011, January). *Educational Leadership*, 68(4).

Fehr-Snyder, K., (2010, August 8). Arizona schools putting more classes online. *Arizona Republic*, 4.

Fullan, M. (2001). *Leading in a culture of change.* San Francisco: Jossey-Bass.

Gabriel, J. (2005). *How to thrive as a teacher leader.* Alexandria, VA: ASCD.

Gardner, H. (1999). *The disciplined mind: What all students should understand.* New York: Simon and Schuster.

Glatthorn, A. (1984). *Differentiated supervision.* Alexandria, VA: ASCD.

Gordon, S. (1991). *How to help beginning teachers succeed.* Alexandria, VA: ASCD.

Gregory, G. & Chapman, C. (2002). *Differentiated instructional strategies: One size doesn't fit all.* Thousand Oaks, CA: Corwin Press.

Hall, T., Strangman, N. & Meyer, A. (2003). *Differentated instruction and implications for implementation.* Wakefield, MA: National Center on Assessing the General Curriculum. Retrieved from http://aim.cast.org/learn/historyarchive/backgroundpapers/differentiated_instruction_udl#.Uthsop6wLYg.

Hassel, E. (1999). *Professional development: Learning from the best.* Oak Brook, IL: North Central Regional Education Laboratory.

Heacox, D. (2002). *Differentiating instruction in the regular classroom: How to reach and teach learners, grades 3–12.* Minneapolis, MN: Free Spirit Publishing.

Heifetz, R. A. & Linsky, M. (2002). *Leadership on the line: Staying alive through the dangers of leading.* Boston: Harvard Business School Press.

Hord, S., Rutherford, W., Huling-Austin, L., & Hall, G. (1987). *Taking charge of change.* Alexandria, VA: ASCD.

Hughes, H. (2009, November). Multigenre research projects. *Middle School Journal*, 40(4), 34–43.

Hunter, M. (1971). *Teach for transfer.* El Segundo, CA: TIP Publications.

Hunter, M. (1982). *Mastery teaching: Increasing instructional effectiveness in secondary schools, colleges and universities.* El Segundo, CA: TIP Publications.

Hunter, M., (1982). *Teach more—faster.* El Segundo, CA: TIP Publications.

Jacobs, H. (1997). *Mapping the big picture: Integrating curriculum and assessment K–12.* Alexandria, VA: ASCD.

Jacobs, H. (Ed.). (2010). *Curriculum 21: Essential education for a changing world.* Alexandria, VA: ASCD.

Jensen, E. (1998). *Teaching with the brain in mind.* Alexandria, VA: ASCD.

Johnson, D., Johnson, R. & Holubec, E. (1988). *Cooperation in the classroom.* Edina, MN: Interaction Book Company.

Johnson, D., Johnson, R., Holubec, E., & Roy, P. (1984). *Circles of Learning: Cooperation in the classroom.* Alexandria, VA: ASCD.

Joyce, B. (Ed.). (1990). *Changing school culture through staff development: The 1990 ASCD yearbook*. Alexandria, VA: ASCD.
Joyce, B. & Showers, B. (1998). *Student achievement through staff development*. London & New York: Longmont.
Joyce, B. & Weil, M. (1972/1980). *Models of teaching*. Englewood Cliffs, NJ: Prentice-Hall.
Katzenbach, J. R. & Smith, D. K. (1993). *The wisdom of teams*. New York: Harper Business.
Lemke, C. & Coughlin, E. (2009, September). The change agents. *Educational Leadership*, 67(1), 54–59.
Lemov, D. (2010). *Teach like a champion: 49 techniques that put students on the path to college*. San Francisco: John Wiley & Sons.
Lenski, S. & Caskey, M. (January, 2009). Using the lesson study approach to plan for student learning. *Middle School Journal*, 40(3), 50–56.
Masci, F. (2008, November). Time for time on task and quality instruction. *Middle School Journal*, 40(2), 34–35.
Marzano, R., Pickering, D., & Pollock, J. (2001). *Classroom instruction that works: Research-based strategies for increasing student achievement*. Alexandria, VA: ASCD.
Marzano, R. J., Waters, T., & McNulty, B. A. (2005) *School leadership that works: From research to results*. Alexandria, VA, Aurora, CO: ASCD & McREL.
Marzano, R. J., Waters, T., & McNulty, B. A. (2009, November). Multiple measures. *Educational Leadership*, 67(3).
Marzano, R. J., Waters, T.,& McNulty, B. A. (2010, February). Meeting students where they are. *Educational Leadership*, 67(5).
Oregon Business Council's Education Roundtable whitepaper (2009). Taking Promising High School Practices to Scale.
Patterson, J. (1997). *Coming clean about organizational change: Leadership in the real world*. Arlington, VA: American Association of School Administrators.
Perkins, D. (1992). *Smart schools: Better thinking and learning for every child*. New York: Free Press.
Platt, A. D., Tripp, C. E., Ogden, W. R., & Fraser, R. G. (2002). *The skillful leader: Confronting mediocre teaching*. Acton, MA: Ready About Press.
Providing positive learning environments. (2007, October). *Middle Ground*, 11(2).
Ready to learn. (2010, March). *Educational Leadership*, 67(6).
Redesigning professional development. (2002, March). *Educational Leadership*, 59(6).
Reeves, D. B. (2009). *Leading change in your school: How to conquer myths, build commitment, and get results*. Alexandria, VA: ASCD.
Reeves, D. B. (2009, February). The learning leader/model teachers. *Educational Leadership*, 66(5), 85–86.
Reimagining School. (2010, April). *Educational Leadership*, 67(7).
Richardson, W. (2009). *Blogs, wikis, podcasts, and other powerful web tools for classrooms*. Thousand Oaks, CA: Corwin Press.
Richardson, W. & Mancabelli, R. (2011). *Personal learning networks: Using the power of connections to transform education*. Bloomington, IN: Solution Tree Press.
Scherer, M. (1999). *A better beginning: Supporting and mentoring new teachers*. Alexandria, VA: ASCD.
Schmoker, M. (1996). *Results: The key to continuous school improvement*. Alexandria, VA: ASCD.
Schmoker, M. (2006). *Results now: How we can achieve unprecedented improvements in teaching and learning*. Alexandria, VA: ASCD.
Scholtes, P., Joiner, B., & Streibel, B. (2003). *The Team Handbook, 3rd edition*. Madison, WI: Oriel.
Seifter, H. & Economy, P. (2001). *Leadership ensemble: Lessons in collaborative management from the world's only conductorless orchestra*. New York: Times Boos/Henry Holt and Company.

Senge, P., Kleiner, A., Roberts, C., Ross, R., & Smith, B. (1994). *The fifth discipline fieldbook: Strategies and tools for building a learning organization*. New York: Currency Doubleday.

Silver, H., Strong, R., & Perini, M. (2000). *So each may learn: Integrating learning styles and multiple intelligences*. Alexandria, VA: ASCD.

Sparks, D. & Hirsh, S. (1997). *A new vision for staff development*. Alexandria, VA: ASCD.

Sprenger, M. (1999). *Learning and memory: The brain in action*. Alexandria, VA: ASCD.

Sprenger, M. (2009, September). Focusing the digital brain. *Educational Leadership*, 67(1), 34–39.

Stiggins, R. & Chappius, J. (2005, January). Using student-involved classroom assessment to close achievement gaps. *Theory Into Practice*, 44(1), 11–18.

Stigler, J. & Hiebert, J. (1999). *The teaching gap: Best ideas from the world's best teachers for improving education in the classroom*. New York: Free Press.

Strong, R., Silver, H., & Perini, M. (2001). *Teaching what matters most: Standards and strategies for raising student achievement*. Alexandria VA: ASCD.

Teaching for the 21st century. (2009, September). *Educational Leadership*, 67(1).

Teaching screenagers. (2011, February). *Educational Leadership*, 68(5).

Tomlinson, C. (1999). *The Differentiated classroom: Responding to the needs of all learners*. Alexandria, VA: ASCD.

Tomlinson, C. (2003). *Fulfilling the promise of the differentiated classroom: Strategies and tools for responsive teaching*. Alexandria, VA. ASCD.

Trilling, B. (2010, April). What does success really mean? *Middle Ground*, 13(4), 8–11.

Unger, C. (1994, February). What teaching for understanding looks like. *Educational Leadership*, 51(5), 8–10.

Wagner, T. (2003). Beyond testing: The 7 disciplines for strengthening instruction. *Education Week*, Commentary, 11/12/2003.

Wagner, T. (2004). The challenge of change leadership, transforming education through "communities of practice." *Education Week*, Commentary, 10/27/2004.

Wenger, E., McDermott, R., Snyder, W. M. (2002). *Cultivating communities of practice: A guide to managing knowledge*. Boston: Harvard Business Press.

Wheeler, M.T., Renchler, R., Conley, K., Summerlight, S. (2000). *National educational technology standards for students: Connecting curriculum and technology*. ERIC 473132. Eugene, OR: International society for technology in education. Published in collaboration with the U.S. Department of Education.

Wiggins, G. (2012). 7 Keys to effective feedback. *Educational Leadership*, 70(1), 11–16.

Wiggins, G. & McTighe, J. (1998). *Understanding by design*. Alexandria, VA: ASCD.

Wormeli, R. (2007). *Differentiation: From planning to practice grades 6–12*. Portland, ME: Stenhouse Publishers and Westerville, OH: National Middle School Association.

Wormeli, R. (2009, February). Failure preferred, actually. *Middle Ground*, 12(3), 39–40.

Zhao, Y. (2009). *Catching up or leading the way: American education in the age of globalization*. Alexandria, VA: ASCD.

ADDITIONAL RESOURCES

Common Core Standards Initiative: Preparing America's Students for College and Career—www.corestandards.org

National Governors Association Center for Best Practices, Council of Chief State School Officers, Common Core State Standards (preface), Publisher: National Governors Association Center for Best Practices, Council of Chief State School Officers, Washington D.C.

Education Week online publications—www.edweek.org

National Commission on Teaching and America's Future—www.nctaf.org

The National Educational Technology Standards (NETS) for Students & Technology Rubrics—http://cnets.iste.org/students/

International Society for Technology Education—www.iste.org

References

George Lucas Foundation—www.edutopia.org

National School Reform Faculty, Harmony Center—www.nsrfharmony.org. Check website as they are in the process of updating, reformatting, and redesigning materials.

Index

academics, 14–18, 24
agents of change, 74–76
American Association of Schools Librarians, 18, 71, 72
ASCD. *See* Association for Supervision and Curriculum Development
assessments: definition for perspective on, 18; formative, 18–19; learning personalized by, 19–20; summative, 18–19
Association for Supervision and Curriculum Development (ASCD), 23

banter, 32
barriers, 30–31
best practices: consideration of strategies for, 53–55; definition of, 53; strategies for establishing, 53–55; team engagement for, 45–46
Blogs, Wikis, Podcasts, and Other Powerful Web Tools for Classrooms (Richardson), 70
bullying, 42, 72

Caroll, Tom, 66
CCSS. *See* Common Core State Standards
celebrations, 55, 76
Chapman, C., 38
Chen, M., 32
classrooms, 39–40, 75
Common Core State Standards (CCSS), 3
communication, 11
communities of practice: goal of transforming teams into, 45–48; identifying areas of study for, 48; perspective on beginnings of, 46; professional responsibilities for, 46, 62; team's determination of best model in, 47
compacting strategy, 54
computers, 34–36
concept: attainment, 54; formation, 54; mapping, 54
confidentiality, 9–10, 11–12
Cookson, Peter, 49
core values, 29, 43, 58–59
Costa, A., 37
Critical Friends, 47
curriculum: school districts' rigorous, 51–52; sharing of rigorous, 15–17; teachers' expertise for rigorous, 16–17; team alignment of, 34–35

Darling-Hammond, Linda, 16–17
digital tools, 35
district mandate, 12–14
Doerr, Hanna, 66
dyad model, 12, 14
Dyak, Brenda A., 35

education: free tools for, 71; inadequacy of traditional practices in, 53; as pedagogical in nature, 3; students as core of, 2, 5–6
educators, 5
emotions, 30–31, 42
empowerment, 76
evaluations, 21–24

feedback, 36; evaluations and concerns of peer, 21–24; instruments for objective, 23–24; leadership growth by peer, 22–23, 24
Four P's for Organized Learning, 36–38; helping teachers with, 43; in Learning Communities, 39; for productive learning environment,

38–43
framework, 27–28
Fraser, R. G., 10
Fullan, Michael, 28

goals: leadership enabling groups to reach, 32; for scheduling training times, 59–60; of team transformation, 45–48
Google, 31, 71
grants, 59
Gregory, G., 38

Harrison, Cindy, 23
honesty, in leadership, 10, 36

independent study, 54
instruments, for feedback, 23–24
intellectual engagement, 42–43
International Society for Technology Education, 77
International Society of Technology Standards, 35

Kallick, B., 37
key lessons, 68–72, 77
Killion, Joellen, 23

leaders, 28, 74–75; control lost at meetings by, 32–34; emotions recognized by, 31; engagement of standards by, 52; frustrations and limits of teacher, 34; job description for teacher, 22, 23; reflections on group by, 28–29; relationships built by, 27–30; responses to parents' challenges by, 17–18; standards supported by teacher, 52–53; teams' issues anticipated by skilled, 30, 43; teams' suggestions heard by, 76
leadership, 10, 34, 77; changes overwhelming, 1, 2–3, 6; as enabling group to reach goals, 32; focus on successful teaching in, 15; peer feedback for growth in, 22–23, 24; PLCs' usefulness identified by, 12–13; power of, 9–12; risk in roles of, 10–11; structure and identification of, 10, 24; teachers' voice of, 62, 63
Leading Change in Your School: How to Conquer Myths, Build Commitment, and Get Results (Reeves), 75
learning, 61, 66, 74; ample time required for professional, 67; assessments balanced for personalized, 19–20; districts unaware of adult's time for, 67; as evident upon students' demonstrations, 50; Four P's for organized, 36–43; importance of team structures in, 65–66; justification of professional teams in, 65–67; as more fluid and complex, 73; organizational structure support for, 4; preferences in, 14; problem-based, 54; productive environment for, 38–43; resource tools' availability for, 71; structures for professional, 12–14; students' increased responsibility for, 74; students' productive, 41–42; teachers' decisions for student, 49–50; teachers' incumbency of creating conditions for, 49; teams' concerns of reduced revenue for, 66; teams defining time for professional, 66–67; technology as tools to support, 34–35; tools found by teams to enhance, 58. *See also* Professional Learning Communities; teaching and learning
Learning Communities' Four P's, 38–43
Lemov, Doug, 40
lesson planning, 40–41
lesson study model, 46–47
Leu, James, 60

mandates and restrictions, 61–62, 63
Marzano, R. J., 3, 10–11
Marzano's taxonomy, 50–51
McNulty, B. A., 10–11
meetings: group leaders losing control at, 32–34; as lines of communication, 11; support sought for control of, 33

metacognition, 56–57
metacognitive strategies, 54
mind's eye, 57
motivation, 55, 75

National Commission on Teaching and America's Future, 66
National Educational Technology Standards for Students, 53
National School Reform Faculty, 43, 47
networks, 34
new normal, 73–74, 75

Ogden, W. R., 10
onion perspective, 1–2, 6–7
organizational structures, 4, 61

pacing charts, 18–21, 24
parents: academics challenged by, 14–18, 24; information nights for, 17; leaders responding to challenges from, 17–18; rigorous curriculum shared with, 15–17; TAG student challenges with, 14–15
pedagogies, 3, 35
Perkins, David, 49
Personal in Four P's, 38–39, 42–43
personal reflection, underestimation of, 57
Pickering, D., 3
Platt, A. D., 10
PLCs. *See* Professional Learning Communities
Pollock, J., 3
powerless feelings, 61–62, 63
Predictable in Four P's, 38–40
principals, 11–12, 21, 24
problem solving models, 31
Productive in Four P's, 38–39, 41–42
Professional Learning Communities (PLCs), 4; district mandate and, 12–14; dyad model transitioning to, 12, 14; leadership identifying usefulness in, 12–13; responsibilities defined for, 13
Purposeful in Four P's, 38–39, 40–41

Reeves, Doug, 32, 75
reflections, 28–29

relationships: framework needed in building, 27–28; issues moved by cultivation of, 30–31; leaders building, 27–30; leaders' role of nurturing, 28; novice teacher to mentor teacher, 37–38; refocusing on purposes of team, 32–33
research, 3–4
resources: availability of learning tools and, 71; core values supported by prioritizing, 58–59; feedback on usage concerns of, 36; time allowances as, 55–57
restrictions. *See* mandates and restrictions
Richardson, Will, 35, 70, 71
risk, 10–11
Rotary Clubs, 59
Rybak, C., 32

safety, 72
school district, 51–52
schools, 1–2, 74
The Skillful Leader: Confronting Mediocre Teaching (Platt, Tripp, Ogden, and Fraser), 10
social media, 57–61
society, 2–3
standards, 61; team engagement by leaders for, 52; team evaluating technology, 35; teams using, 51–53; technology, 68–72, 77
students, 2, 4–5, 37, 50; assured access of technology for, 68–69; challenges with parents of TAG, 14–15; classrooms' diversities of, 75; engaged learning of productive, 41–42; ensuring engagement of, 1; as heart of educational endeavor, 5–6; learning responsibilities of, 74; new normal for success of, 73–74; online safety for, 72; pacing charts to best serve, 20–21; problem solving encouraged in, 16; safety needs of, 42; teachers' decisions for, 49–50; technologies as significant in lives of, 57–58, 62–63; technology as tool for engaging, 68
success, 4–5

support, 33

talented and gifted (TAG) students, 14–15

teachers, 61, 62; behavior expectations of, 34; changes required in traditional roles of, 73; computer access replacing, 34–36; difficult undertakings for beginning, 40–41; as *doing with* rather than *dealing to* students, 37; expertise on technology content by, 69–70; Four P's for helping, 43; frustrations and limits of, 34; induction of new, 36–38; leaders acknowledging importance of, 75; leadership's focus on successful, 15; leaders' job description for, 22, 23; learning conditions incumbent on, 49; learning teams inducting new, 66; lesson study model to improve, 46–47; pedagogical implications understood by, 35; relationships of novices with mentoring, 37–38; as reluctant to ask for help, 48; rigorous curriculums' expertise from, 16–17; standards supported by leaders of, 52–53; student learning decisions by, 49–50; university-public schools partnership supporting first-year, 47; voice of leadership by, 62, 63

teaching, 15; responsibility expected in technology, 71–72; teachers authorized for enhancements in, 61; for transfer in problem-solving, 54

teaching and learning: defining, 48–51, 62; evolving paradigm in, 73–74; new normal as result of shift in, 74, 75; reasons for defining, 50–51; team discussions illuminating complexity of, 48–49, 62; technologies supporting, 59

teams, 45–48, 52, 58; agents of change and empowerment of, 74–76; approaches to curriculum alignment by, 34–35; best practices by engaging, 45–46; communities of practice by, 47; emerging strategies' benefits of, 67; justification of professional learning, 65–67; leaders anticipating issues of, 30, 43; leaders listening to suggestions of, 76; learning and importance of structuring, 65–66; moving beyond emotions of, 30–31; new teachers inducted by learning, 66; reduced revenue concerns for learning, 66; relationships refocused on purposes of, 32–33; standards used by, 51–53; teaching and learning discussions of, 48–49, 62; technology standards evaluated by, 35; time defined for professional learning by, 66–67; usage of emerging technologies and social media, 57–61; validation of individual's work in, 29–30; work grounded by core values of, 29, 43

technologies, 2–3, 34–35; expectations for responsible use of, 71–72; key lessons' commonality of, 72; professional training for evolution of, 70–71; as significant in students' lives, 57–58, 62–63; standards of, 68–72, 77; students' assured access of, 68–69; teachers' content expertise for, 69–70; teaching and learning supported by, 59; teams using social media and emerging, 57–61; technophobes using web-based tools for, 60–61; as tools for engaging students, 68

technophobes, 60–61

testing/pacing disagreements, 18–21, 24

test scores, 18, 48

time, 57, 67; districts unaware of adult's learning, 67; resource of taking, 55–57; schedules for training, 59–60; teams defining professional learning, 66–67

Tripp, C. E., 10

trust, 9–10, 11–12

university-public schools partnership, 47

Wagner, Tony, 46–47

Waters, T., 10–11

About the Authors

Jan Burgess spent twenty-four years in school administration, as an elementary and middle school principal following eight years as a teacher and counselor. Her work with teachers and teacher leaders over those years framed her understanding of shared leadership, what it takes to create a culture to sustain learning, and how teaching practices impact learning. Jan has experienced firsthand the synergy that develops in vibrant learning environments for students and what it takes to make learning irresistible.

Jan earned her bachelor's degree in Elementary Education from Lewis and Clark College in Portland, Oregon, and a master's degree in Guidance and Counseling from Portland State University. She has credentials in Administration and Educational Leadership. In 2005, after thirty-two years in public education, Jan retired and now focuses her work as a consultant and mentor to new principals.

An author, Jan has published numerous articles in educational journals and two books:

1. *A Smart Start to Professional Development: From Sticky Notes to Dragon Boats, 20 Slightly Off Kilter Activities for Middle Schools* (2008, NMSA).
2. *Other Duties as Assigned: Tips, Tools and Techniques for Expert Teacher Leadership* (2009, ASCD).

Jan Burgess can be reached at 6120 SW Chestnut Avenue, Beaverton, Oregon, 97005 or at jbb2@comcast.net.

Donna Bates has over thirty years of elementary and middle level teaching experience. During her years of teaching, Donna served as an elementary team leader, middle level curriculum leader, and teacher association president and was a participant on a number of district and state committees.

She earned her B.S. degree at the University of Oregon and has since completed graduate-level work at Lewis and Clark College, Portland State University, and the University of Oregon.

While designing differentiated learning options for students in content areas, Donna designed a program entitled "Voices of Injustice" which was recognized by the National Middle School Association as being one of four exemplary programs in the nation for 2001.

Other Duties as Assigned: Tips, Tools and Techniques for Expert Teacher Leadership written by Jan Burgess with Donna Bates was published by ASCD and released in December 2009.

Donna's personal teaching style has always centered on providing differentiated instruction for students in her classroom. Her personal goal has been to validate and support academic achievement for all students.

Donna can be reached at 2528 E. Indigo Brush Rd. Phoenix, Arizona, 85048 or at batesd10@Yahoo.com.